NURTURING THE UNBORN CHILD

NURTURING THE UNBORN CHILD

A Nine-Month Program for Soothing, Stimulating, and Communicating with Your Baby

by Thomas Verny, M.D.,
and Pamela Weintraub

Delta

A Delta Book
Published by
Dell Publishing
a division of
Bantam Doubleday Dell Publishing Group, Inc.
666 Fifth Avenue
New York, New York 10103

ISBN: 0-385-30673-3

Reprinted by arrangement with Delacorte Press

Manufactured in the United States of America

Published simultaneously in Canada

June 1992

10 9 8 7 6 5 4 3 2 1

RRH

CONTENTS

Part Three

The Third Trimester

HOW THIS BOOK CAME ABOUT

One of the most frequent questions I am asked is how I became interested in the psychology of babies and pregnancy. It happened through my psychotherapeutic work. As a psychiatrist, I would, every once in a while, witness a client spontaneously regressing to an earlier time in his or her life. Sometimes an individual would actually seem to go back to birth or even to the womb. This invariably occurred without drugs or hypnosis—without my leading the client in any way at all.

I still vividly remember one of the first incidents, though it happened more than fifteen years ago. In the midst of discussing his dream, Paul, my twenty-five-year-old patient, changed his expression, curled up like a little baby, and started to sob. After about ten minutes he came out of this state and told me that he had just experienced himself lying in his crib and crying for his mother. Then, being a skeptical young professional, he said, "You know, I must be making this up because I saw myself in a white crib just now and yet I have seen pictures of myself as a baby taken in a blue crib."

I suggested that Paul discuss the matter with his mother. At his next appointment I was astonished to hear that according to his mother, he spent the first two months of his life in a borrowed *white* crib. His parents later bought him his very own crib, which was blue. The same crib was in all the photos he recalled.

As I continued to witness this sort of flashback in patient after patient, I began to question the accepted academic notion that babies do not remember anything before the age of two. To see whether my doubts were founded, and whether the very early memories I recorded were in fact real, I began an extensive six-year search of the scientific journals of the world. I read everything I could find in the area of embryology, with particular emphasis on the development of the nervous system and the hearing of the unborn child. I also collected clinical case studies of adults reliving post- and prenatal traumas—especially painful experiences that could be traced to events occurring during and even before birth. On the basis of this huge compilation of data, I wrote, with John Kelly, *The Secret Life of the Unborn Child,* published in 1981.

I have continued working in this area by founding the Pre- and Perinatal Psychology Association of North America (PPPANA), serving as its president from its inception to the present. I also started the *Pre- and Peri-Natal Psychology Journal,* the official scientific publication of PPPANA, and served as editor for four years.

In the course of hundreds of radio, television, and newspaper interviews, as well as public lectures, I was always asked the same question: What practical measures could pregnant women take to implement the principles I proposed in *The Secret Life of the Unborn Child.* Another frequently raised concern was the pregnant mother's ability to deal with the stresses of pregnancy and relate to the father of the child.

These issues were very much on my mind when, in the winter of 1989, I met Pamela Weintraub, editor-at-large of

Omni magazine. She was writing an article on pre- and perinatal psychology and had come to interview me in Toronto. Following the interview, we had several more telephone conversations about issues related to the article, and Pamela suggested that perhaps we could write a book together on babies. The mother of two small children, she had profound respect for the intellectual and emotional development of the unborn, something that appealed to me. What's more, sharing the load of writing would save us both a lot of time, a commodity always in short supply. Finally, in the spring of 1989 we sat down to write a straightforward, practical guide to help mothers and fathers soothe, stimulate, and most important, love, the unborn.

—THOMAS VERNY, M.D.

I remember sitting behind my editor's desk at *Omni* magazine in the early 1980s and reading the latest material on prenatal psychology. I was skeptical, to say the least. Not yet a mother myself, I questioned whether a baby still in the womb could possess the emotional sensitivity or sheer intuitive power to grasp anything about the mother's inner or outer life.

All that changed in 1983, when I became pregnant myself. The tiny baby in my womb—now my first son—was obviously sensitive to my emotional state. In fact, because I was often anxious during this pregnancy, my child registered my emotions in a particularly powerful way. When I was calm, he seemed to lie peacefully, making tiny, gentle movements every now and then. When I worried about his health, which I often did (needlessly, I now know, because he was perfect), I felt the movements strengthen. And one night, when I thought we would be forced to give up our apartment, I felt my baby rush from side to side for hours with the wild abandon of a monsoon.

The birth was complex as well. After fourteen hours of labor, the doctor decided my baby was just plain stuck and performed a cesarean. That was fortunate, because it turned out I'd had a streptococcus B infection; the infection could have caused serious damage in a vaginal birth. But because of the fever the infection gave me, the hospital wouldn't let me hold my baby for almost a week. I should have been ecstatic with my beautiful, healthy little boy, but I couldn't help feeling upset at being able to see him only from a distance, through the nursery glass.

My second pregnancy was far easier and less anxious than the first. After all, I now knew how irrational it was to worry about a few allergy pills, aspirin, and beers consumed before I even knew I was pregnant. We lived in a secure, pleasant place. My second baby moved consistently but calmly; he was a gentle, reassuring, life-affirming presence within. After the birth, also a cesarean, I was able to keep my baby by my side.

I now believe that my two sons, the products of two different pregnancies, have been at least partially influenced by their experience in the womb and immediately after birth. My firstborn, Jason, is at once exquisitely sensitive and a hothead. He has a tremendous creative drive: For instance, he was *writing* his own small books in kindergarten. He cries at the sad parts of movies. Not yet seven, he endlessly ponders the deeper issues: birth and death, the origin of people and stars. Yet he is quick to anger, becoming indignant if he even suspects a slight.

My second child, David, is steadier and more intrepid. Independent and self-possessed at the age of two, he insists on doing everything himself, from fastening his car seat to pouring his drink to carrying his books and toys. He routinely climbs to the top of his dresser and jumps to the floor without pause. A loving child, he easily gives and receives hugs and kisses. And his adjustment to a playgroup in which I would not be present was smooth indeed.

It was soon after the birth of David that I began to consider the implications of pre- and perinatal psychology once more. I was, I now realized, open to the ideas of this discipline in a powerful way. I had just finished writing a couple of how-to books with a psychologist, and so it was only natural for me to think of creating one based on pre- and perinatal psychology as well. If only, I thought to myself, I had had such a book, how much easier my own two pregnancies might have been.

In the winter of 1989, after I met Thomas Verny, the prime mover of this field in the United States and Canada, I hoped I could persuade him to work on a book that would address my concerns. Dr. Verny was immensely knowledgeable, and perhaps that's why he had realistic, achievable, important goals. He did not care to try to create little Einsteins—something neither of us believed in. Rather, he hoped to make the pregnancy experience a period of love and communication between expectant parents and the unborn.

I would not change my own two children in any way. Yet, I wish that during my pregnancies I had had access to the program we ended up creating for this book. I know it would have helped to reduce my level of anxiety, benefiting myself and my children. I also know I could have used these techniques to keep in touch with my husband's feelings and take more control over my experience while giving birth.

I do not plan to have any more children. But I almost wish I could, just for the chance to experience pregnancy as it should and can be—the calm, confident, and joyous beginning of a new relationship, an inner journey toward personal exploration and growth.

—PAMELA WEINTRAUB

INTRODUCTION

Tell a pregnant woman that her unborn child hears her voice or senses her love, and she's bound to agree. For mothers intuitively know what scientists have only recently discovered: that the unborn child is a deeply sensitive individual who forms a powerful relationship with his or her parents—and the outside world—while still in the womb.

Now that you are pregnant, you may well have joined the ranks of women who understand the importance of communicating love and acceptance to the child you carry within. These days, science has a lot to add to that understanding. The latest research validates your feelings, showing just *how* unborn children see and hear, remember, and perhaps even think. In recent years, researchers have also used the new knowledge to develop a series of specific, highly effective techniques to help you communicate with the unborn. Presented here in our special program, called the Womb Harmonics System, these techniques will enable you and your spouse or partner to nurture a sense of calm, thus soothing your unborn child and preparing him for a life of confidence and ease. As you sing to, dance with, and massage your baby, you will stimulate his nervous system and communicate your love. And as you talk to, dream about, and even visualize your unborn child, you will strengthen your life-long bond, making your pregnancy a time of enormous joy and growth.

The abilities of the unborn and the potential for parents to strengthen the prenatal bond have long been described by mothers themselves. One woman we know, Sara, says that during her pregnancy she followed a simple routine. Each evening after her husband went to bed, she performed her Lamaze breathing exercises while watching *M.A.S.H.* reruns on TV. "The *M.A.S.H.* theme became a signal for me to relax," Sara explains. "I forgot the tensions of the day—including the problems between my husband and myself—and I felt truly happy."

As early as six months after her son was born, Sara noticed that he would stop whatever he was doing and stare at the television whenever the theme song to *M.A.S.H.* came on. "He is now two years old," Sara says, "and no matter where he is or what he's doing, when that song comes on he stops and stares, almost as if he's in a trance. Every time this happens, my husband and I are amazed."

And another mother, Ashley, recalls the day when, sitting around the dining-room table, she joked about the pajamas she'd frequently worn while pregnant with her little girl. "Do you remember those pajamas, Susie?" she asked the three-year-old.

Susie's answer amazed the family. "I couldn't see what you were wearing. I could only hear what you were saying," she replied.

"What did it feel like?" Ashley asked.

"It felt dark and crowded, like a big bowl of water."

"What was your favorite food?"

"I didn't get any food."

"What did you think when you were born?"

"It wasn't crowded anymore," Susy replied. "I could stretch."

"The astonishing thing," Ashley explains, "is that she described the entire experience without ever saying she had *seen* anything. She described only what she had heard and felt. She never slipped or answered a question wrong."

Still another mother, Emily, who is a grade-school art teacher, reports that her two-year-old was unusually deft at drawing faces; perhaps most surprising, the young artist *automatically* put eyes, ears, nose, and mouth in the correct location on the face. Emily marveled at her young child's uncanny skill—until she remembered that during her pregnancy, she had verbally and explicitly instructed her grade-school class to render the human face again and again.

These stories make sense in light of startling new research conducted throughout the United States and Europe during the past two decades. Unborn children, dozens of university and hospital studies show, can see, hear, feel, and perhaps even form a rudimentary level of awareness in the womb. What's more, psychologists now contend, prenatal life and the birth experience are often profound determinants of human personality and aptitude. Countless musicians, for instance, were exposed to music during gestation. And time and again, psychologists have traced such qualities as self-confidence, depression, and addictive behavior to experiences in the womb.

The Nine-Month Program

Every parent would like to be able to use such findings to optimize the emotional and intellectual potential of his or her own children. This book was written to help you do just that. It offers a simple, step-by-step program based on our own Womb Harmonics System. This program features scientifically effective exercises for relaxing prospective parents and nurturing and stimulating the unborn child up to, during, and immediately after birth.

As you begin to apply our system, you will, first of all, relax yourself, eliminating or reducing the production of stress hormones such as adrenaline and noradrenaline, which may flow across the placental wall to reach your unborn child. As you advance through your pregnancy, and the Womb Harmonics System, you will also stimulate your baby, communicating your presence through his still-unfocused sensory capabilities. The exercises in this volume will also help initiate a form of psychological communication, letting your unborn child know she is truly wanted and loved.

The nine-month program will help you enhance your own emotional fitness as well. Exercises designed to increase your self-awareness and your intimacy with your spouse will strengthen the family unit into which your baby is born. The notion of a strong, harmonious family is a crucial part of our program—in fact, the sense of peace, harmony and togetherness is the element from which the moniker *Womb Harmonics* comes. If the pregnant mother and her partner are full of tensions, anxieties, and concerns, it will be hard for them to find time and energy for the baby. If they are constantly fighting with each other, their relatives, and the world, it will be hard for them to give the love that their child so desperately needs. Just as a woman who wants to become pregnant must make room in her womb for the new being, she and the father must make room in their minds and hearts for the child they desire to have.

Most other pregnancy books and programs focus on the physical aspects of pregnancy and childbirth. They warn pregnant mothers not to drink alcohol or caffeinated beverages and not to take drugs. They emphasize a well-balanced diet, with adequate amounts of calcium, iron, and protein and lots of fruits, vegetables, and grains. Pregnant women reading these books are advised to exercise in moderation and get plenty of rest.

All these suggestions are, of course, vitally important. But the Womb Harmonics System goes beyond these physical matters. Our program allows you to explore the *inner emotional experience* of your pregnancy. During the course of our own work with patients, we have found that most people approach pregnancy in one of three ways: as a dire crisis, as something to be endured, or as an opportunity for personal growth. This book is intended for all three groups, but if it is used correctly, it will help members of the first two groups change affiliation and join the ranks of the third. No matter what group you start out in, you will find within the exercises of Womb Harmonics an *interactive program* that *empowers* you with *personal control* over your pregnancy from beginning to end. We hope that during the high-stress period that pregnancy has become for many in today's world, you will find our book a trusted friend.

Though this book's *nine-month* program is designed to carry you through the course of your pregnancy, the benefits you accrue should last a lifetime. From increased self-knowledge and self-esteem to enhanced relaxation and focusing skills, you will learn to master potent psychological techniques for coping with many aspects of life. Needless to say, the advantages gained by your child will persist as well. The Womb Harmonics baby is likely to enter the world with increased alertness and curiosity, a powerful sense of harmony, and the knowledge that he is loved.

Why the Program Works

Our goals may be ambitious, but they are *not* farfetched. In fact, the research on which our book is based has recently given rise to a whole new discipline: *pre-* and *perinatal psychology,* the neurological and psychological study of babies before and during birth. This burgeoning medical specialty is already represented by its own professional, peer-reviewed journal *(Pre- and Peri-Natal Psychology Journal),* and its own societies (including the International Society for Prenatal and Perinatal Psychology and the Pre- and Perinatal Psychology Association of North America, or PPPANA.) The floodgate of research is creating a totally new picture of the unborn.

Indeed, back in the days of Freud, experts believed that personality did not even *begin* to form until age two or three. During the 1960s, psychologists traced early emotional development to the hours and days after birth, formulating the concept of *bonding*—in which mother and child establish attachment and communicate their love immediately after the baby emerges from the womb. But to most psychologists, the notion that elements of personality were actually formed by the experience of gestation seemed absurd. Until the moment of birth, experts held, the human fetus was a blank slate, lacking true sensation, emotional affect, or even the ability to feel pain.

Pre- and perinatal psychologists, however, have recently proven the existence of significant sensory capabilities in the womb. Thanks to clinical tools such as ultrasound, for instance, scientists peering into the womb have shown that by the fourth month after conception the unborn child has a well-developed sense of touch and taste. He will suck if his lips are stroked. If a bitter substance like iodine is introduced into the amniotic fluid, he will grimace and stop swallowing liquid. At the same age, the baby can perceive a bright light shining on the mother's abdomen; if the light is particularly bright, he will even lift his hands to shield his eyes.

At five months, the same child will react to a loud sound by raising his hands and covering his ears. In a series of remarkable studies conducted during the early eighties, moreover, University of North Carolina psychologist Anthony DeCasper showed that the unborn baby even has the capacity to perceive and remember sounds of speech, to recognize a story heard repeatedly in utero, and to recognize his own mother's voice.

In addition to these amazing sensory abilities, the baby in the womb may actually experience what we think of as "consciousness"—a rudimentary awareness of himself and the world beyond. While it is impossible to pinpoint an unborn child's thoughts for certain, research conducted by neuroscientist Dominick Purpura of New York's Albert Einstein Medical College shows that the baby in the womb has formed the brain structures necessary for learning and even awareness sometime between the twenty-eighth and thirty-second weeks of development. To reach this conclusion, Purpura removed brains from premature infants born of miscarriage and studied them under the microscope. Editor of the highly respected journal *Brain Research,* Purpura found that the cerebral cortex—the seat of thought—is almost as developed during the eighth and ninth month of gestation as it is after birth.

Other researchers studying babies in the womb seem to bolster these findings. For instance, scientists measuring brain waves found that unborn children experience periods of wakefulness and periods of sleep. Further studies show that babies in the womb exhibit the physiological measurements associated with dream sleep. It is impossible, of course, to prove that the unborn child actually dreams. But the similarity in brain function between the unborn child and the adult suggests that our essential humanity may be with us *very* early.

It's no wonder, then, that prenatal psychologists see the very core of human personality forming not during the first three years of life, but, rather, in the womb. Studies show that this personality formation takes place through intensive communication between parents—especially the mother—and the unborn. In one telling study conducted by a pediatrician in Switzerland, for instance, it was found that babies literally absorbed the sleeping habits established by their mothers during pregnancy. Without any particular training, for instance, babies born to early-rising mothers invariably rose early; those born to late-rising mothers generally went to bed late.

In another study showing how signals from the mother influence the experience—and perhaps the nature—of the child in the womb, Austrian obstetrician Emil Reinold asked pregnant women to rest under an ultrasound machine for about thirty minutes. Responding to the mother's relaxed state, the babies began to relax too. At a certain point, each mother was told that her baby had stopped moving. (True, since the baby was so relaxed.) Of course, that information terrified the mothers, inducing a surge of adrenaline. Responding to the mothers' signals, the babies—all in view on the ultrasound screen—began kicking up a storm.

Obviously, part of the response was *physiological.* We all know that everything the mother eats, drinks, or inhales is passed through her bloodstream into the body of her baby. That is why smoking, drinking, and drugs should be avoided during pregnancy. But research like that conducted by Reinold proves that maternal *emotions* are transmitted physiologically as well. If a pregnant mother experiences acute or chronic stress, her body will manufacture stress hormones (including adrenaline and noradrenaline) that travel through her bloodstream to the womb, inducing the same stressful state in the unborn child. Though some stress during pregnancy is normal, our studies show that mothers under extreme and constant stress are more likely to have babies who are premature, lower than average in weight, hyperactive, irritable, and colicky. In extreme instances, these babies may be born with thumbs sucked raw or even with ulcers.

The babies in Reinold's experiments responded not just to their mothers' surge of adrenaline, however, but also most likely to the mothers' *behavior.* Behavioral communication takes place through the mother's activities—when she pats her stomach, talks, sings, or dances, the unborn child knows that mother is actively there. (This level of communication may include the father and other family members as well.) The baby, in turn, responds by kicking and moving about. Just as the mother of a newborn quickly learns to distinguish the baby's cry of "Good morning, feed me," from, "Hey, get that pin out of my behind!" so the pregnant mother can learn to differentiate between happy and distressed kicking.

One instance of behavioral communication was discovered by audiologist Michele Clements, who hoped to convince a prospective father that his unborn child could truly *hear.* Clements asked the father to place his head up against his wife's pregnant abdomen and yell. Each time the father yelled, the unborn child expressed his extreme annoyance by sharply kicking the wall of the womb. In fact, if behavioral messages are loving and consistent, parents can establish a nurturing back-and-forth dialogue with the unborn that may continue long after birth.

Such communication, established through mothers' and

fathers' behavior, is usually accompanied by interaction on the *psychological* plane. By psychological communication, we mean the baby's ability to respond to his or her mother's deepest feelings and thoughts. Babies pick up on the emotional charge carried by spoken language as well as unspoken attitudes and affects. When a mother strokes her baby through her abdomen, and says, "How are you, how is my wonderful baby," the baby senses that she is loved and that makes her feel good. We as adults thrive on love, praise, and respect. Children, born and unborn, do as well. In one recent study, for instance, women who deeply wanted their babies had the easiest pregnancies and healthiest offspring; those who did not want their babies had more medical problems as well as more instances of low birth weight and premature and emotionally disturbed infants. This study and others indicate that thoughts which infuse the developing baby with a sense of happiness or calm can set the stage for a balanced, happy, and serene disposition throughout life.

Profound parental and environmental influence also occurs during and immediately after birth. In anecdote after anecdote, the newborn seems to sense gentleness, softness, and a caring touch. He responds to these things far differently than he does to bright lights, electrical beeps, and the cold, impersonal atmosphere so often associated with medical birth.

In one dramatic example, a Seattle pediatrician was treating a desperately ill baby in his hospital's neonatal intensive care unit, or NICU. Hooked up to a battery of life-support machines, the baby was flooded with light and exposed to more sound than you might hear on Fifth Avenue at rush hour. The child was just not getting enough oxygen, and he was turning blue. The doctor decided the infant was going to die anyway, so he took him off life-support systems, shut off all the machines, and turned off the lights. Then he took the baby out of the crib and rocked him in his arms. Within a few minutes the baby turned pink, and his recovery was complete.

The experience of birth is so far-reaching, in fact, that recent studies link especially difficult or traumatic births to suicide and some forms of drug addiction. Psychologist Lee Salk, for instance, found that teenage suicide was more prevalent in those whose mothers lacked prenatal care or were chronically ill during pregnancy. Other research suggests the existence of bona fide birth *memories.* California obstetrician David B. Cheek has shown that people retain a muscle memory of the way their heads, shoulders, and arms moved as they entered the world. And psychologist David B. Chamberlain, also from California, has collected what he believes are detailed and literal memories of birth: Chamberlain's patients, in fact, report vivid, movielike recollections of doctors, delivery rooms, and conversations dating back to the first few minutes of life.

As the research shows, unborn and newborn children are sensitive, intuitive, emotive individuals. With significant perceptual and mental capabilities, they *truly* experience gestation, sustaining, in some sense, at least, a memory of in utero development and birth. These earliest experiences, research indicates, shape human personality as profoundly as subsequent life events. Therefore, if you do your best to remain calm during your pregnancy, if you communicate a sense of love to your unborn baby, and if you orchestrate a joyous, positive birth, you will be contributing immensely to the emotional and physical health of your child for the rest of his life.

Techniques and Strategies

Based on this cutting-edge research, the special exercises in the Womb Harmonics System can help you experience the best possible pregnancy for you and your child. Our step-by-step plan will teach you a number of deep-relaxation techniques to help you quell your anxiety and maintain a physiologically balanced state of calm. At the same time, a different set of exercises will help you boost your energy when pregnancy hormones—and the simple strain of carrying a baby—get you down.

The Womb Harmonics System can also help you defeat negative thought-styles, anxieties, and fears. You will, for instance, learn to resolve conflicts, coming to terms with your spouse, your parents, your childhood, and your friends. With our exercises to guide you, you will even visualize your own birth, grasping, perhaps for the first time, the meaning of the birth experience for you. You will also face the negative thoughts that emerge from time to time during your pregnancy. As you face these thoughts, you will be able to let them go. In their place, you will construct a positive, life-affirming point of view.

Perhaps most important, the Womb Harmonics exercises can help you and your unborn child establish a powerful bond. By using such natural communication tools as speech, music, and movement, you and your partner will let your unborn child know that you are *there* for her. And through visualization and guided imagery, you will discover powerful images of your baby, enhancing the sense of intimacy between you and the unborn.

In short, the Womb Harmonics System can help you resolve your own emotional conflicts and teach you and your mate to soothe, stimulate, and communicate with your unborn child in a loving, systematic, scientifically effective way. From song and dance to dream work and guided imagery to yoga and massage, the Womb Harmonics parent will use effective psychological tools to enhance the experience of pregnancy and nurture the unborn.

The basic Womb Harmonics tools include:

- *Journal writing.* We'll show you how to keep a journal for venting your most private thoughts. Using the journal, you can explore your feelings about pregnancy, learn to overcome body image problems, and confront deep-seated fears.
- *Dream work.* At the beginning of the program, we will show you how to record and interpret your dreams so that you can get in touch with your hidden feelings. Then you will learn advanced techniques for inducing emotionally positive dreams; such dreams will immerse your unborn child in a soothing hormonal sea, resulting in sensations of acceptance, calm, and love.
- *Deep relaxation.* You will learn to enter the state of *alert progressive relaxation,* in which the body descends into a sleeplike state while the mind remains acutely alert. This altered state of consciousness is particularly important not only because it promotes deep and refreshing relaxation but also because it makes the mind more receptive to images.
- *Visualization.* While you are in the receptive state of deep relaxation, you can use visualization to invoke powerful images that enhance the well-being of your baby. In one visualization exercise, for instance, you will imagine your child immersed in healing waters and the energizing rays of the sun. In another, you will simply see your unborn child and feel especially close.
- *Guided imagery.* To guide you through the more complex visualization exercises, we will show you how to make

your own guided-imagery tapes. These tapes will help you experience and relive aspects of your own childhood, infancy, birth, and intrauterine life. They will also help you form a bond with the unborn.

• *Music.* You'll record your own music tapes, and we'll show you how to use them to help you relax, intensify your powers of visualization, and stimulate the unborn.

• *Partner dialogues.* A series of specific, probing questions we pose will help you and your partner participate in directed conversations. These are aimed at helping you sort out your deepest feelings and strengthen your relationship.

• *Affirmations.* Practiced in some form or another by many behavioral therapists, an affirmation is a positive thought planted in the conscious mind. By repeating an affirmation over and over in highly specific ways, you can eventually become more open to the positive suggestions within. At the same time, negative thought-patterns that are at odds with the affirmation will be understood—and eventually erased.

• *Tactile stimulation.* As your baby grows, you can learn to communicate with her through touch. By patting and rubbing the womb and doing other tactile exercises, in fact, you can initiate a dialogue with the unborn. As you massage and touch your abdomen, you will enhance your baby's feeling of being loved, contribute to her sense of self-esteem, and, according to recent research, even accelerate the development of her peripheral nervous system.

• *Verbal stimulation.* After a certain point in the pregnancy, your unborn child can recognize your voice. By talking to the developing child in a caring, systematic way, you can go far in forging a two-way path of communication between you and your baby.

• *Free drawing.* In one of the most important Womb

Harmonics techniques, you will generate images directly from your unconscious. Using plain white paper and crayons, you will get in touch with your true feelings about your unborn child and even stir some long-forgotten memories of your own birth.

• *Mandala drawing.* By drawing *mandalas*—ancient Buddhist circlelike figures that stimulate a sense of balance and the ability to focus inward—you can achieve insight into the deepest layers of your unconscious.

• *Claying.* By closing your eyes and playing with a piece of clay, you may get in touch with your own birth experience and develop a greater sense of closeness to the child within.

• *Rhythmic breathing.* Extensive research has proved beyond doubt that rhythmic breathing causes complex, beneficial physiological changes, including an improved supply of oxygen to the blood, more efficient brain functioning, and better disposal of bodily wastes. Eastern yogis have made a science of the rhythmic breathing technique, developing hundreds of different exercises, each one geared to achieve a particular goal. In the Womb Harmonics System, you will learn a few of the more relevant methods and in the process boost your energy, deepen your relaxation, and enhance your inner concentration.

How to Use This Book

The Womb Harmonics exercises will evolve and change along with your needs and the needs of your baby. Some exercises are meant to be repeated throughout the nine-month period, while others will be restricted to a particular trimester. Still others will be conducted only once. For instance, relaxation techniques are continued throughout the nine months, but verbal communication with the unborn child is emphasized only after the five-month mark, when the baby's hearing apparatus is fully functional.

The program itself is organized in a clear and straightforward way. Each month of your pregnancy has its own chapter, consisting of an introduction and a series of exercises related to that segment of prenatal development. To make your progress through the program as easy as possible, each exercise has a name and a number for easy reference. And a descriptive box at the beginning of each exercise summarizes the exercise. Each summary box includes:

- the exercise *theme,* which defines the goal of the exercise
- the *instruments,* or tools, you will use during the exercise. These may include anything from a prerecorded musical tape to pencil and paper to clay.
- a list of *participants* who will engage in the exercise. These may include you, your partner, your unborn child, and any children you may already have.
- the *tempo,* or the time the exercise takes and the frequency with which it is to be performed.

For instance, in "Viva Vivaldi," our exercise on stress reduction through music, the descriptive box looks like this:

THEME: Stress reduction through music
INSTRUMENT: Music tape
PARTICIPANTS: Mother and unborn child
TEMPO: One hour, at least twice a week, for the duration of the pregnancy

Finally, so that you will have an adequate overview as you proceed, each chapter ends with three charts. The first summarizes your exercise program for the month; the second details your baby's prenatal development; and the third describes the physical changes in you.

In an ideal world, a bell would have gone off the moment you conceived. But as it is, it is hard to know the moment when pregnancy begins. Most home pregnancy tests do not show a positive result until ten days after a missed period. Even laboratory tests do not reliably indicate pregnancy until ten days after conception. In many, if not most cases, women do not realize they are pregnant until after they have missed at least one period. And most women do not realize they are pregnant until two to six weeks have gone by. So it may be impossible for you to start our program on the month—let alone the day—your pregnancy begins.

If you do embark upon our program after the first month of pregnancy, simply start at the beginning and work your way through. If you are between six and eight weeks pregnant when you begin, we suggest that you spend about two weeks learning the core exercises presented for Month One of pregnancy. Then spend the next five weeks integrating the exercises presented in Months Two and Three. If you are more than eight weeks pregnant, you may go through the exercises a bit more rapidly, proceeding at your own pace until you catch up. But you need not rush yourself or feel that you must do every single exercise to make this program work for you. As long as you keep the emotional well-being of both yourself and your unborn child uppermost in your mind, you will derive full benefit from the exercises no matter when you begin.

Whether or not you follow our system from your first month of pregnancy, feel free to adapt the program to your own special interests and needs. For instance, if you are a visual person as opposed to a verbal one, you might emphasize communicating your feelings through pictures rather than words. If your energy level is low, you might make more use of the energy-boosting techniques; if you feel irritable and tense, you might find that the relaxation exercises are tailor-made for you.

You also need not feel compelled to do every single exercise. When we devised our program, we decided to err on the side of abundance. Use as many or as few of our exercises as you like, as frequently as you like. Look upon this book as a smorgasbord of techniques. *You* decide what you want to put on your plate.

Indeed, the Womb Harmonics System is not a rigid program that must be followed to the letter to work. Rather, the program is meant to interact, in an ongoing fashion, with *your* specific needs and goals. When used successfully, the Womb Harmonics exercises can help you set the appropriate internal conditions for your emotional growth and self-understanding. They will enable you to overcome emotional blocks as you communicate your love and affection to your unborn. But the exact regimen you follow is up to you and your personal predisposition.

You will find that many of the Womb Harmonics exercises are appropriate for your partner as well. For the longest time, men have been left out of the pregnancy experience. But social norms have changed drastically over the last twenty years, and now, men want to be involved in as many phases of pregnancy and birth as possible. Your partner may already plan to attend prenatal classes to assist in the labor and birth. With the guidance of exercises in Womb Harmonics, he can become a full participant in your pregnancy right from the start.

No matter how you and your partner choose to adapt our exercises for yourselves, we suggest that you try to avoid thinking of your unborn child as a boy or a girl—unless, of course, the baby's sex has been determined by amniocentesis. Instead, we encourage you to think how much you'll love your baby and to focus on having a healthy baby regardless of gender. To help you with this, we'll refer to the unborn child alternately as "he" or "she." Notice that we use "he" in the odd-number months and "she" in the even-number months throughout the book.

We emphasize the importance of a positive outlook, but please do not be jarred or disturbed by fleeting worries, doubts, or anxieties. These are a normal part of every pregnancy. They will have no adverse effect on your baby. If you follow our exercises faithfully, even your persistent doubts and fears should fade.

You are now ready to embark upon your journey into the world of Womb Harmonics. We wish you and your baby a joyful, enriching pregnancy and a wonderful relationship throughout your lives.

PART ONE

The First Trimester

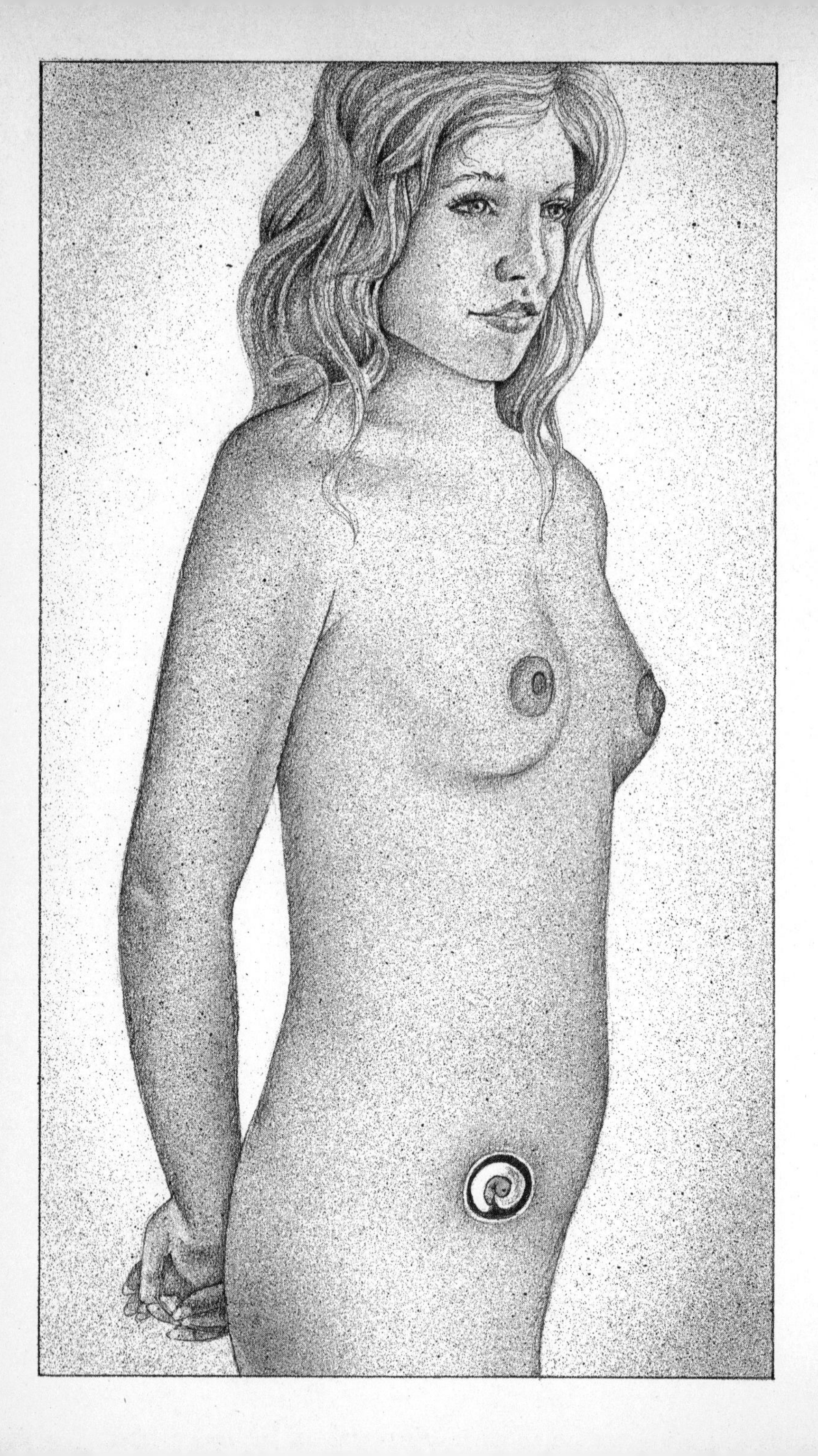

1

MONTH ONE: In the Beginning

You're going to have a baby! The news fills you with a rush of emotion—a sense of wonder, perhaps, or sheer exhilaration and joy. Mixed with these feelings, however, may be sentiments of doubt, insecurity, and fear. Pregnancy imbues most women with a range of emotion. The sooner you get in touch with *all* your feelings, the smoother your pregnancy will be.

In our experience, nothing gives a child a more solid foundation in life than the experience of being loved and wanted in the womb. Ideally, all children should be conceived in tenderness and carried to term with adoration. Life does not always work this way. But even if your pregnancy has come as a surprise, even if it threatens to disrupt your life, your unborn child needs your love as much as you need air to breathe and food to eat. Because the unborn child requires affection and attention from both parents, you and your partner should emphasize positive feelings whenever you can.

To help you remain calm and tune in to your deepest feelings, you can listen to audio tapes featuring classical music. Researchers have pointed out that baroque music—including compositions by Bach, Corelli, Handel, Mozart, and Vivaldi—moves to the tempo of sixty to seventy beats per minute, a rate very close to that of the resting human heart. Impressed by this fact, Bulgarian psychiatrist Georgi Lozanov played music by Mozart for his students, and it increased their powers of concentration. Other researchers have shown that Baroque music stimulates alpha waves, the brain waves associated with alert concentration and a sense of calm. Finally, British audiology expert Michele Clements has discovered that most unborn children shift to a state of alert relaxation when they are exposed to the Baroque compositions of Mozart and Vivaldi. On the other hand, when they hear long orchestral pieces by Bach, Brahms, and Beethoven, they demonstrate anxiety in the form of increased kicking and accelerated heart rate. (The same negative reaction is also triggered by hard rock music and the unpleasant sound of a pneumatic drill.)

Given these findings, the first Womb Harmonics exercise, "Viva Vivaldi," provides a musical program geared to strengthen your capacity to visualize and relax. At the same time, the music we recommend (recorded on audio tapes by you and your spouse or a friend) will calm your developing child, possibly stimulating brain cells required for concentration and learning later in life.

To help you unwind and tune in to your innermost thoughts, "Time Out for Mom" (Exercise 2), teaches you the technique of *alert progressive relaxation,* in which your body enters a sleeplike state while your mind remains alert. As you learn to enter and sustain this potent state of consciousness, you will rid yourself of bottled-up anxiety and become progressively more receptive to positive images and thoughts.

Exercise 3, "Daily Diary," shows you how to give vent to your feelings by writing in a journal. You can use your journal to express your private thoughts and honestly confront your anxieties and fears.

You can also use your journal to help you practice the "Affirmations" of Exercise 4. Affirmations help you replace negative thought-patterns with a positive, empowering, hopeful outlook. As you practice the affirmation technique, you may discover self-defeating, negative thought-patterns that prevent you from achieving your full potential. After you recognize these negative thoughts and discover what may be causing them, you can use our affirmation exercise to help you embrace a healthier, happier point of view.

Finally, the fifth exercise, "Dream Work," will help you explore your dreams, revealing your hidden thoughts and feelings. Though you may not remember your dreams, research indicates that you have them about four or five times a night. Virtually all psychologists believe that they provide a road map to your unconscious mind. Sigmund Freud viewed dreams as an outlet for repressed sexual and aggressive drives, but modern evidence suggests they serve a positive, healing function as well. By remembering, understanding—and to some degree modulating—your dreams during pregnancy, you can work to resolve many of your internal and interpersonal conflicts.

Whether you are recalling your dreams or writing in your journal, think of Month One of the Womb Harmonics System as a journey into yourself. If practiced faithfully, the five exercises that follow can help you marshal your resources and personal power. They can also bring to light hidden concerns and worries; by resolving these outstanding issues, you will help yourself become the best parent you can be.

The psychological techniques you will be mastering during your first month of pregnancy are much like a pianist's scales. Just as a pianist must practice her scales over and over if she wants to maintain her virtuoso skills, so too, you must learn to relax and get in touch with your feelings and those of your partner if you are to move through pregnancy with aplomb and ease. Once you master these basic techniques, we recommend that you practice them for a few minutes every day of your pregnancy.

We also suggest you introduce Month One techniques in a systematic and orderly way. Make sure you feel comfortable with the music and alert progressive relaxation exercises before you initiate the daily journal-writing activity. When you feel confident about the journal-writing portion of your day, expand that activity to include affirmations and dream work.

Ideally, you should wait three to four days after working with one technique before you progress to the next. Remember that the techniques introduced in Month One will become integral parts of your daily life. If you try to bite off too much at once, you may feel overwhelmed. In fact, if you do not have a chance to integrate all five Month One exercises into your life during your first month of pregnancy, don't worry—just work them into your schedule during the month that follows. If you take the program slowly, you will be rewarded with a sense of ease and confidence that should carry you, your partner, and your baby through the next nine months.

TIPS FOR BUSY MOTHERS

If you already have children or a job outside your home, you may not have the time for every single exercise in this book. For already busy and overextended mothers, we suggest utilizing periods of "lost time" that are essentially wasted. Examples of these underutilized moments include driving your car, riding a bus, waiting for an appointment at the doctor or dentist, taking a bath, walking, gardening, or cooking. You can probably think of many others. The trick is to fill these periods of lost time with appropriate exercises. For instance, you can write in your journal on the subway or listen to a guided imagery tape while taking a bath. You can also be selective about the Womb Harmonics techniques that you ultimately tap. After reading all the exercises appropriate to your baby's age, select the ones you feel will benefit you, your baby, and your mate most. We consider the five exercises presented in Month One to be essential. Please do not skip these. Apart from these bedrock techniques, feel free to pick and choose from subsequent exercises without feelings of guilt. Do what you can and you will be giving your baby a head start.

Exercise 1: Viva Vivaldi

THEME: Stress reduction through music
INSTRUMENT: Music tape
PARTICIPANTS: Mother and unborn child
TEMPO: Sixty minutes, at least twice a week, for the duration of the pregnancy

Before you begin this exercise, choose sixty minutes of music that you find particularly relaxing and enjoyable. Because the slow movements of Baroque and Baroque-like composers most resemble the rhythm of the resting maternal heartbeat that the fetus hears in the womb, we suggest you use this type of music. We particularly recommend composers such as Haydn, Boccherini, J. S. Bach, Mozart, Handel, Fasch, and Vivaldi. Some of the more appropriate compositions include Schubert's "Trout" Quintet in A Major for Piano and Strings, Vivaldi's Guitar Concerto in D, Largo, Mozart's Piano Concerto No. 21, Handel's Harp Concerto in B-Flat, and Vivaldi's Flute Concerto in D. If you would like a tape made specifically for pregnant mothers, we suggest *Love Chords* by Thomas R. Verny and Sandra Collier (see Resource Guide).

If you don't like classical music, any music that puts you in a relaxed mood—with the exception of hard rock or acid rock—will do. Women who have attended rock concerts during pregnancy say that they felt their unborn child moving wildly in response to the music. One pregnant woman worked as a technician in a recording studio where a rock band was cutting a record. During the rehearsals, her baby became upset and finally kicked her so hard that he broke one of her ribs. On the other hand, you should not choose music that is *too* soothing or flat. Lullabyes, elevator music, and some of the New Age compositions may put you—and possibly your baby—right to sleep! This is not the desired effect at all. You want to use the time during which the music is playing to commune and communicate with your baby, and you can do so only if both of you are awake. Appropriate nonclassical selections might include Paul McCartney, James Taylor and Judy Collins.

If you choose to make a tape that features a variety of artists, try to make the transitions from one selection to the next smooth and natural. Since the aim of this exercise is relaxation, you won't want to disrupt the mood you've established.

Once you have chosen your sixty minutes of music, record your selection or selections on a cassette tape. Listen to this tape whenever you please; we suggest that you listen to it in its entirety at least twice a week. If at all possible, find two quiet periods a week when you can simply sit in a comfortable position and, as your mind wanders, listen to the tape straight through. Don't lie down while playing this special tape—that may cause you to fall asleep, defeating the goal of conscious *relaxation. And don't use this tape as background music while you are working or driving. The idea of this exercise is to totally and actively focus your attention on the music to the exclusion of all other things.*

Special Note: At the end of your ninth month, while your baby is being born, take this tape into the delivery room and play it during labor. It will help you and your baby to relax —and it will probably help your partner and your birth attendants as well. After birth, you may find that when your child is sick or fretful, playing this special tape will help him to relax and feel better.

Exercise 2: Time Out for Mom

THEME: Deep relaxation
INSTRUMENT: Alert progressive relaxation tape
PARTICIPANT: Mother
TEMPO: Twenty minutes, once a day, for the duration of the pregnancy

You can reduce stress during pregnancy by regularly achieving states of deep relaxation. By truly relaxing, you will not only make your pregnancy more enjoyable, you will actually reduce the amount of adrenaline and other stress hormones that are produced by your body, ultimately reaching the child inside. Researchers have shown that anxious mothers who generate excessive amounts of adrenaline have babies who seem jumpier and cry more often than others. Some of these babies were even born with duodenal ulcers. On the other hand, women who are relatively calm during pregnancy often have calmer babies, not to mention easier births.

Alert progressive relaxation is perhaps the most effective relaxation technique ever devised. It is used extensively by sports psychologists who wish to help athletes concentrate and improve their performance, as well as by behavior therapists who understand that relaxation is a crucial part of achieving goals. The technique enables you to relax your body completely while your mind remains sharp and alert. As you take "time out for Mom," your muscles will loosen, your breathing rate and heart rate will slow, and after about twenty minutes, you will feel refreshed and reenergized, ready to resume your day.

Before you actually master the technique of alert progressive relaxation, there are a few things you will need: A comfortable chair and a footstool or ottoman on which you can prop your feet; a tape recorder and a cassette tape for recording exercise instructions, to which you will listen in the future; ten minutes of relaxing music; and a second tape player or other music source, from which you can record your chosen musical selections. We suggest that you take your favorite ten-minute segment from the music tape you made in "Viva Vivaldi" and use it for this exercise as well. You may, however, use any musical selection that conforms to the guidelines established in Exercise 1.

After you have gathered these tools, please prepare your tape machine so that you can record the instructions given below. Your partner or a close friend may read the words into your tape recorder for you; we have found that the voice of a trusted friend or lover is particularly effective. But if you prefer, you can read the instructions yourself. We suggest that the person who reads these instructions read them over silently before actually making the recording. When ready, the reader should strive to read the script below slowly and calmly, *pausing where appropriate.*

> *Close your eyes and take a couple of deep breaths. Continue to breathe* deeply *and* evenly, *allowing yourself to focus on the rhythm of your breathing, on your bodily sensations, and on any feelings and images you have about yourself. If thoughts about the outside world intrude, just let them pass, the way clouds pass over the horizon. Notice them, and then let go of them.*
>
> *Now become aware of your* feet. *Notice the pressure on them and the angle at which they are placed. Become aware of the soles of your feet. No-*

tice your heels, *your* toes, *your* ankles. *Now begin to curl your toes toward the soles of your feet, as if trying to make contact. Push your toes* down, down, down. Hold *them, and then let go.*

Breathe in and out. Relax and let go.

With each breath that you take, you are choosing to go deeper *and* deeper *into a perfect state of relaxation. You are not falling asleep. You remain alert but relaxed.*

Now become aware of your legs, *from your knees down to your ankles. As you become aware of your legs, I want you to tighten all your leg muscles. Tighten, tighten, tighten.* Hold. *And relax.*

Breathe in and out. Relax and let go.

With each breath that you take you are going deeper *and* deeper *into yourself, and your body is becoming more and more relaxed.*

Now focus your attention on the middle of your body—your thighs, *your* pelvis, *and your* buttocks. *As you become aware, tighten all the muscles in these areas. Tighten, tighten, tighten.* Hold. *And relax.*

Breathe in and out. Relax and let go.

Continue to breathe deeply and evenly. With each inhalation, you are breathing in fresh oxygen and fresh energy. With each exhalation, you are breathing out carbon dioxide and bodily wastes. Think of each inhalation as a way of taking in love and support from the universe. Think of each exhalation as a means of ejecting negative feelings and tension.

Now go on to the next section of your body. Become aware of your spine *from your pelvis to the base of your head. Begin to press against the back of your chair or supporting cushions along the length of your spinal column.* Push down, down. *Now* hold *that position. And let go. Feel your back and your chest going limp.*

Breathe in and out. Relax and let go.

Each breath that you take helps your body to relax. Whenever you inhale, every muscle, each individual cell, is nourished and energized. Whenever you exhale, every muscle, each individual cell, is cleansed of impurities and tensions. Your body and your baby are really enjoying this exercise.

Now become aware of your shoulders *and your* neck *and all the tension that you store there. Begin to wash out this tension by pushing the tips of your shoulders up toward your* ears; *push until you feel as if you can almost touch your ears with your shoulders.*

Push, push, push. Hold *it. And let go.*

Breathe *in and out. Relax and let go.*

Now lift your hands a few inches above your body and make a fist. *Tighten your fist.* Tighten, tighten, tighten. Hold. *And let go.*

Breathe in and out. Relax and let go. Continue to breathe deeply *and* evenly. *With each breath that you take, you choose to become more relaxed. You feel comfortable and safe and secure.*

Now become aware of your face. *Notice the muscles around your eyes, your mouth, and your jaw. Begin to squint your eyes. Tighten the muscles around your mouth. And tighten your jaw.* Tighten, tighten, tighten. Hold. *And let go.*

Breathe in and out. Relax and let go.

Now that your body is relaxed, your mind should be relaxed as well. The music will start in a few

> *moments. Listen to the music and let it take you wherever you need to go. Just drift. Don't work at it. You deserve to relax. You need it, and your baby needs it.*
>
> *After you have finished the musical section of this tape, you will feel relaxed and revitalized.*

Immediately after these instructions on the tape, please record your ten-minute music selection. After the music has been recorded, have your reader follow it up with the rest of the script:

> *Now slowly return to a state of complete waking consciousness. First wiggle your fingers and toes. Now open your eyes. Remember to preserve your new sense of calm. Still relaxed, use all your senses to focus on your immediate surroundings. Now, refreshed, revitalized, and relaxed, you may get up and continue with your day.*

Once you have created your tape, you may practice the alert progressive relaxation technique. First, choose a twenty-minute period of time during which you know you will not be disturbed. Then go to a quiet section of your home, sink into your comfortable chair, and start the tape. Please follow the instructions to the best of your ability without analyzing them; try to let the words, images, and music carry you away.

Special Note: In the beginning, you should use this technique for relaxation only. But as your pregnancy—and the Womb Harmonics System—proceeds, you will find that alert progressive relaxation makes it easier for you to explore your relationship to your own body, your unborn child, and the events of your past. You will also use the alert progressive relaxation technique as a lead into the guided-imagery exercises, in which taped instructions enable you to establish a closer bond to the child growing within.

Exercise 3: Daily Diary

THEME: Increasing self-understanding
INSTRUMENTS: Notebook and pen
PARTICIPANT: Mother
TEMPO: Once a day, for the duration of the pregnancy

One of the most powerful tools for exploring your feelings during pregnancy—or any time at all, for that matter—is a daily journal. Staying in touch with your emotions is particularly important during pregnancy, when your life is changing before your eyes and when your feelings may be especially intense.

To begin your journal-writing activity, buy any kind of a notebook that appeals to you. It may be a simple student exercise book or a silk- or leather-bound diary. If you wish, you may also purchase a special "journal-writing" pen; we suggest a felt-tipped pen that you can use even when lying down. Since you will also use your journal to record dreams, you may find the ability to write while still in bed particularly important after first awakening. You may also wish to have a penlight for easy writing in the dark.

Store your notebook in a safe place. Don't leave it just anywhere in your home—this journal is your personal property, for your eyes only. Consider it your friend and confidante, and trust it with your innermost secrets as well as your most outrageous desires and ideas. If you write in your journal almost every day, as we suggest you do, you will achieve a better appreciation for who you are and how you feel about yourself. You will also come to terms with feelings, both positive and negative, concerning your parents, your partner, and motherhood itself.

As you recognize and assume responsibility for your feelings, you will develop the capacity to make positive changes in your life. For instance, you may gradually realize that you fear the burdens of parenthood—or the loss of intimacy with your partner. As you come to terms with these feelings, you will be able to work them through. The result will be enhanced self-awareness that will encourage you to communicate with your partner or even formulate long-range life goals. As you process your hidden anxieties and insecurities, your self-confidence, your sense of optimism, and your mental outlook will improve. Remember, your mental outlook contributes to your baby's inner world. The unborn child is intimately connected to your body, which is deeply affected by the things you think and feel. A preponderance of negative feelings may have a negative impact on your baby, while positive feelings will be life-enhancing.

To start your journal, find a quiet time when you will have at least fifteen or twenty minutes to yourself without being disturbed. We suggest that you choose a room that has ample lighting and good ventilation, and that you avoid areas where you may hear a TV or a radio playing in the background.

Begin your first entry simply by putting the date at the top. As you write, be completely honest about what's on your mind. But please try to focus on your emotions—examine your fears and anxieties, your periods of joy and contentment. Especially during the first month of your pregnancy, you should record any events or personal interactions that provoked you into strong positive or negative feelings. Has a fight with your boss or a local bank teller enraged you? Are you particularly happy about a political coup at the office, a new friend, or a simple walk by the lake? Record it here. Keep in mind that you are doing this for yourself—your sentences don't need to be grammatically perfect. And don't worry about spelling. Just get your thoughts and feelings down on paper as completely as possible. You may also doodle or draw, or paste in funny stories or cartoons from the newspaper. Whatever seems relevant to you *should go into your journal.*

As part of the journal-writing activity, flash back to your childhood. If a TV show reminds you of the time you ran away at age five, record that memory in as much detail as possible. What provoked the incident? How did you feel? What were you wearing at the time? How was the situation resolved? And does it continue to affect you today?

Special Note: As your pregnancy progresses, you will use your journal more and more extensively. The next two exercises, introduced during Month One and then expanded upon throughout this book, teach you to affirm positive thoughts and understand your dreams. As you carry out these techniques, as well as others to be introduced in the coming months, you will use your journal as an aid.

Exercise 4: Affirmations

THEME: Raising self-esteem
INSTRUMENTS: Affirmations and journal
PARTICIPANT: Mother
TEMPO: Two minutes, twice a day

A friend named Joan felt particularly troubled by her past. After she was born, it seems, her mother had become very depressed and had continued to suffer bouts of depression for years. When Joan became pregnant, she feared that her fate would be the same after the birth of her own child. To help her work out this fear, she repeated the following statements to herself again and again: *I am a sane person totally grounded in reality; I will be a strong and competent mother;* and *The birth of my baby will fill me with joy.*

These simple statements eased the fears of this mother-to-be. They are known as affirmations—positive thoughts that help one focus on a desired end. Affirmations may be used repetitively, much like the mantras associated with yoga. But these deceivingly simple "thought bites" do not simply drum canned and appropriate notions into your head. Nor do they merely minimize or suppress negative thoughts, like painting over a crack in the ceiling instead of repairing the leak in the roof. Rather, the affirmation technique helps you to locate and defuse the original negative message, usually embedded in your mind at a very early age.

To discover the negative thought-patterns you have stored in your unconscious, first read the statements listed below.

- *I am a very competent person.*
- *I like myself.*
- *I am lovable.*
- *I am loving.*
- *I am capable of unselfish love.*
- *I am a person with opinions of my own, and I understand that others have a right to personal opinions as well.*
- *I have the right to say no to people without losing their respect or love.*
- *I am honest.*

- *I am in touch with reality.*
- *The negative aspects of my past relationships do not determine the way in which I relate to people now.*
- *I am creative and resourceful.*
- *I am self-reliant and independent.*
- *I can think clearly in times of stress.*
- *I can take charge in a crisis.*
- *I am true to myself.*
- *I can assert myself in the presence of anyone.*

Examine this list, and choose the affirmation that seems most appealing. You need not feel that the affirmation describes you, but rather, that you would like it to be true. If you would like to create an affirmation of your own, please feel free to do so. Then turn to a blank sheet of paper in your journal and write the date and the title "Affirmations" on top. Fold the page in half, lengthwise. On the left-hand side, write the affirmation you have chosen. Each time you write the affirmation, include your own name in the statement. For instance, if you have chosen the first affirmation on the list and your name is Michelle, you would write, I, Michelle, am a very competent person. *Make sure that as you print the statement, you* feel *its meaning as deeply as possible. You might also repeat the affirmation aloud.*

After you have printed your affirmation, turn to the right-hand side of the paper and record your reaction to the affirmation, whatever it may be. If you fear the affirmation is not true, explain why. If the thought of living up to the affirmation fills you with anxiety, shame, or guilt, express this as best you can. Then write the same affirmation again in the left-hand column, followed by your reaction again on the right. For instance, if you have chosen the affirmation I, Michelle, am a very competent person, *you might arrange your journal page as follows:*

1/1/91, Affirmations

I, Michelle, am a very competent person.	*The hell you are! What about the time you spent an hour driving back and forth looking for that hotel you booked along the shore?*
I, Michelle, am a very competent person.	*Oh, yeah? Then why were you given such a small raise at your last salary review?*
I, Michelle, am a very competent person.	*Then why are you afflicted with so much self-doubt?*

And so on. Take each affirmation through ten or twenty repetitions. As you write, notice the changes in your response from one repetition of the affirmation to the next.

As you express doubts, as shown in the column at right, you will actually be exploring your negative thoughts. If unexplored, these negative thoughts might simply continue to upset you. But once you verbalize your doubts, you should be able to ease them—even if you initially agree with the doubts expressed. Eventually, the negative thoughts should subside and the positive feelings expressed by the affirmations should hold sway.

Please remember that affirmations work by purging negative thought-patterns and replacing them with positive ones. However, new thought-patterns often require changes in behavior; you must be willing to change not only your outlook, but also your actions and reactions in the real world before the impact of the affirmation exercise is complete.

For instance, it is not enough to *say* you are competent: You must walk, talk, and act as if you feel competent. Likewise, it is not enough to say you are loving: You must act lovingly to those who count.

We suggest that starting today, you work with affirmations daily. Practice the affirmation technique every day, but work with no more than three different affirmations a week. The affirmation technique is most effective if practiced first thing in the morning or just before going to bed at night. But if you feel particularly low or discouraged during the day, take some time out for affirmations at that point as well.

After you have worked with an affirmation for about a week, stop using the response column and simply write the affirmation statement or repeat it aloud. After all, once you have come to grips with your negative beliefs, there is no point in perpetuating them.

During the first month of your pregnancy, affirmations should focus on self-esteem. Thus, whether you use the affirmations we present or create one of your own, for the next four weeks your statements should relate to this issue.

If you do decide to create your own affirmations, here are some guidelines:

- Statements of affirmation should be as simple and concise as possible.
- All affirmations should be phrased in the present tense. For instance, say, *I am able to feel good about my appearance as my pregnancy advances,* instead of, *I will feel good about my appearance when my pregnancy advances.*
- All affirmations should be phrased in a positive way. Say, *I can express my feelings to others,* as opposed to, *I will not repress my feelings.*

Finally, before you begin, here are some extra tips that you may choose to integrate into your own affirmation regime:

- Write your chosen affirmation on a card and put the card on your night table, desk, bathroom mirror, or any other place where you can see it often during the day.
- If an affirmation is particularly important, repeat it out loud for five minutes in the morning, five minutes during the day, and five minutes at night for an entire week.
- Say affirmations aloud while looking in the mirror. As you repeat your affirmation, strive for a confident and happy expression on your face.
- Create a cassette tape with a series of affirmations. On the tape, repeat each affirmation slowly, about ten times. You may play this recording while driving to the office, gardening, or exercising.

How will you know when the affirmation technique has been successful? When negative responses no longer come to mind, and the affirmations you are working with become completely integrated into your point of view and way of life.

Special Note: The affirmation technique introduced here is an integral part of the Womb Harmonics System. While the first month of pregnancy focuses on self-esteem, affirmations in subsequent months will help you deal with your feelings about pregnancy and the life developing within you. We will also present affirmations for the expectant father and ones that prospective parents can do together.

Exercise 5: Dream Work

THEME: Probing the unconscious
INSTRUMENTS: Dream journal and dreams
PARTICIPANT: Mother
TEMPO: Every time you recall a dream

Though many people do not remember their dreams, everyone has them—usually one every ninety minutes, four or five times a night. Freud called dreams "the royal road to the unconscious," and that assessment is as true today as it was when he first formulated the idea. Our dream images reveal how the unconscious views what is going on in our waking lives and in our bodies.

Freud considered dreams an outlet for repressed sexual and aggressive drives, but many experts today believe that dreams may also help the dreamer solve problems, heal the psyche, and enhance spirituality. A dream may express hidden conflicts, but it may also highlight unrecognized talents or neglected aspects of personality that require attention if the dreamer is to grow.

To learn and grow from your dreams, you must understand what they mean. Dreams, like poetry, make use of metaphor; if you understand the metaphors, you will understand the meaning behind your dreams.

Dream symbols vary from person to person, but experts now say that during pregnancy, certain dream symbols may be more prevalent than others. In one study of pregnant women and dreams, for instance, psychologist Patricia Maybruck found an abundance of architectural structures, animals, and water images. The architectural structures usually represent the womb; the animals usually represent the fetus; and the water usually represents the notion of pregnancy and birth. In keeping with the scale of the first trimester, the animals may be tiny lizards or small furry puppies, kittens, or bunnies. The architectural structures may include small cottages and bungalows or even single rooms. And the water may appear in the form of a bath or a pond. Second- and third-trimester women might dream of tigers, skyscrapers, and oceans.

Please do not worry if, after studying your dreams, you find they express more anxiety than you had expected. Studies prove that pregnant women do show more anxiety in their dreams than other women. Researchers have even discovered that *some* anxious dreaming may be a positive thing: In one study, women who expressed the most anxiety in their dreams delivered babies in less than average time. Women who expressed the least anxiety in their dreams took the longest to deliver their babies, while women who fell into the middle range of anxiety were also intermediate in the length of their labor. The implication? Women who express anxiety in their dreams are somehow getting their feelings out, psychologically preparing themselves for the experience of birth.

Start your dream work by remembering and recording your dreams. You will first need a dream journal. You may want to use the journal you have already started, or you may prefer to have a separate dream journal. A simple notebook, one that can be easily stored under your pillow, is best. Since you may wake up and remember many of your dreams in the middle of the night, you may wish to keep a penlight or flashlight nearby. After you have gathered your special dream-recording tools, store them under your pillow and tell yourself, This is where I will record my dreams.

To encourage dream recall, during some quiet part of your

day you might carefully observe your surroundings and imagine them incorporated into the fabric of a dream. Then gently tell yourself, Tonight I will remember my dreams. *After this brief interlude, go on with your day. At night, before you fall asleep, again tell yourself,* Tonight I will remember my dreams. *By repeating this simple phrase for the duration of your pregnancy, you will find that your ability to recall your dreams is dramatically increased.*

Keep in mind that some dream memories may be fleeting. So when you wake up in the morning or in the middle of the night with dream images still flowing through your mind, try to capture them in whatever way feels most comfortable for you. Many people do this by lying still with their eyes shut for a few minutes after they wake up. After they recall the dream, they record it in their journal. Others take out their dream journal and begin to write at once. Whatever method you choose, make sure that as you describe your dream, you depict the setting, the cast of characters, and any other details, no matter how unimportant they may seem. Write about the emotions your dream has triggered and the meaning you believe it has. If you like, draw or doodle in your dream journal.

After you have recorded a dream in your dream journal, add the date and time. You may also want to give each dream its own title. If you want to analyze your dreams, now is the time to do so. If you are open and honest, you will know what the dreams mean for you.

Month One Summary

1. Viva Vivaldi	Music to grow by	60 minutes, twice weekly

2. Time Out for Mom	Relaxation	20 minutes, once a day
3. Daily Diary	Writing	Every day, as needed
4. Affirmations	Positive thinking	At least 2 minutes, twice daily
5. Dream Work	Understanding dreams	Every time you have a dream

Your Baby at One Month Gestation

WEEK	DAY	SIZE	EMBRYOLOGICAL AND FUNCTIONAL CHANGES
1	2	microscopic	4–8 cells
	3		A 16–32-cell raspberry-shaped ball
	5		A hollow sphere of about 150 cells
2	7	.01 in. (.33 mm)	Embryo implants on uterine wall.
	12		Placenta begins to form.
3	18		Nervous system begins to develop.
	20	.06 in. (1.8 mm)	Foundation for the brain, spinal cord, and peripheral nervous system and rudiments of eyes are formed. The first blood vessels appear, and the heart is delineated.
4	28	.25 in. (6 mm)	The building blocks for 40 pairs of muscles develop. Thirty-three pairs of vertebrae appear. The heart begins to beat. The body, as long as diameter of

a standard pencil lead, consists of a head, a trunk, a tail, and tiny arm buds. The mouth opens, and slow, generalized movements of the head, trunk, and extremities occur in response to stimulating the skin. The placenta is fully functional.

Please Note: The baby's age used here is the actual or "embryological age." Obstetricians and many books use "menstrual age," which assumes that the baby was conceived two weeks after the last menstrual period. Consequently, there may be slight discrepancies in weight and size between what's presented here and what you may encounter in other books.

You at One Month of Pregnancy

WEEK	THE PREGNANCY EXPERIENCE
1	Your egg is fertilized about two hours after sexual intercourse.
2	Human chorionic gonadotropin is produced, evoking a positive response on a blood pregnancy test.
3	At the beginning of the third week, you should miss your first period.
4	At twelve days to two weeks after your first missed period, home urine tests may reveal a pregnancy (80% accurate).

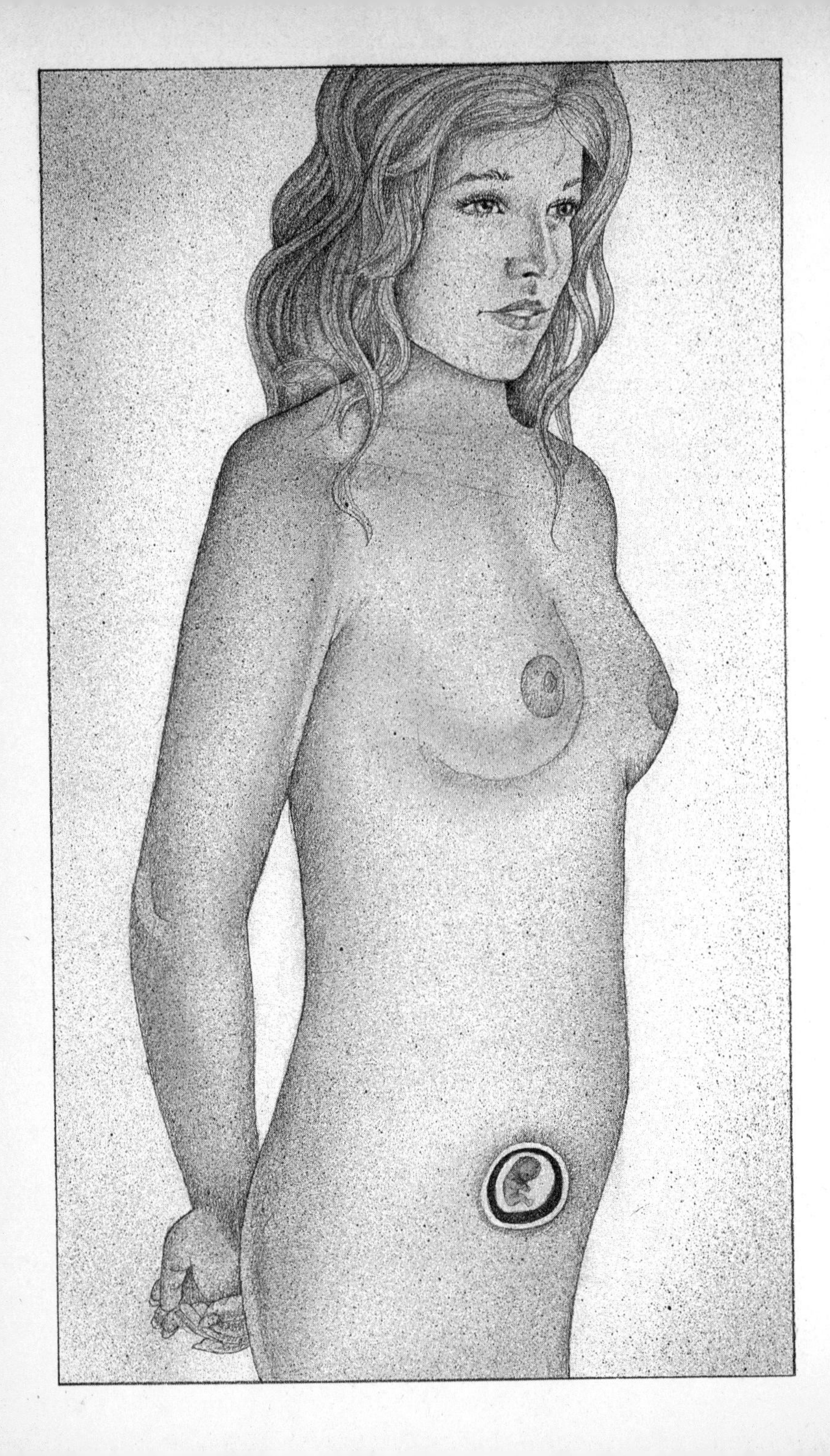

2

MONTH TWO: Tilling the Garden

During your second month of pregnancy, you will find yourself awash in a sea of hormones. As your pregnant body produces elevated levels of estrogen and progesterone, you will probably feel more tired than usual. Many women feel nauseous, dizzy, and exhausted—as if some powerful tranquilizer had been pumped through their veins. The hormonal surge is also changing the way you feel: Your altered chemistry renders you especially sensitive to your own feelings, to the moods of others, and to the world.

Thanks to this heightened sensitivity, you will find yourself increasingly receptive to the language of intuition. This open, intuitive bent should make you particularly deft at this month's goal: fertilizing the soil of the womb with positive thoughts and images. The sooner you feel completely comfortable about the new life forming within, the sooner you will be able to cultivate the soil in which it can flourish and grow.

Since your baby is growing inside you day by day, Month Two is a good time to start communicating with her. By conveying your love and devotion to the developing child at this early stage, you will begin to establish a crucial bond.

To help you fight off the exhaustion the surge of hormones may bring, we present a creative visualization technique called "Feast on a Star" (Exercise 6), in which you fix particularly potent high energy images in your mind.

Creative visualization, introduced this month to boost your energy, will become an increasingly important part of our pregnancy program as time goes on. The technique, in which you create and concentrate on powerful visual images, has helped cure disease, enhance performance, and improve state of mind. Used by ancient medicine men, shamans, and yogis for millennia, visualization was long the first line of defense against disease. With the advent of modern medicine, based on chemical and physical cures, mental imaging fell out of favor.

Recently, however, a mounting body of scientific evidence has emerged to suggest that mental imaging can have a wide-ranging impact on body and mind. For instance, Carl and Stephanie Simonton, a radiation oncologist and a psychotherapist, respectively, are convinced that attitudes and feelings can have a strong impact on health. The Simontons developed a series of mental imaging techniques to augment traditional cancer therapy. Patients treated at the Simonton Cancer Counseling and Research Center in Dallas, Texas, now have a recovery rate twice the national average.

The use of visualization techniques to improve physical and mental performance has been embraced by sport psychologists as well. Colorado State University psychologist Richard M. Suinn, for instance, has his athletes enter a state of alert progressive relaxation. After his charges are deeply relaxed, they produce what Suinn calls a "controlled dream"—a state that combines the deep concentration and imagination of the dream with the awareness and control of the waking state. Immersed in this altered state, Suinn's athletes—including U.S. Olympians in Nordic skiing, the biathlon, and the pentathlon—visualize their events from beginning to end. The method improves their performance so much, Suinn says, "that in one study of Alpine skiers, trained subjects performed so much better than the control group that the coach never really gave the control group skiers a chance to compete." In the Womb Harmonics program, you will use similar imaging techniques to soothe your nerves, to penetrate your deepest feelings, and to prepare you for the effort of labor and birth.

You will also spend much of Month Two resolving outstanding psychological issues, including any negative feelings left over from childhood. It is a truism in psychology that many of life's difficulties stem from our relationships with our parents. In times of stress, unconscious problems become magnified and disturb us more. Pregnancy is certainly a time of stress, and if you want to ease your feelings of uncertainty while moving through this difficult period, learning and growing in the process, you must confront the baggage of your past.

To aid this process, you will spend a good deal of time working with your journal. In Exercise 8, "The Right-Brain Spin," you will express your deepest thoughts and feelings. In Exercise 9, "Home Truths," and Exercise 10, "Snapshots," you will remember the events of your childhood through both directed and stream-of-consciousness writing. You will also spend time dealing with the way in which your parents have taught you to view childbearing and childrearing. Through journal writing and dreamwork, you can come to terms with the unconscious mental programs you have absorbed. And with the help of the affirmation technique, you will learn to rewrite these programs long before your baby is born.

In the last exercise presented this month ("The Pregnant Pause" Exercise 11), you will learn to resolve any doubts you have about your pregnancy. This is important since positive maternal emotions have been shown to advance the health of the unborn child. Nowhere is this clearer than in a study conducted by University of Salzburg psychologist Gerhard Rottman back in 1974. Rottman studied 141 women, dividing them into four categories of maternal suitability, from ideal (women who deeply wanted their children) to catastrophic. The women he labeled ideal had the easiest pregnancies and deliveries and the healthiest offspring. Those labeled catastrophic had the most extreme medical problems during pregnancy and the highest rate of low-weight, premature, and emotionally disturbed infants. His most interesting findings, however, concerned the two intermediate groups. In one group, the mothers claimed they were thrilled to be having babies, but Rottman's psychological tests—and, apparently, the babies themselves—detected something wrong. These mothers unconsciously feared having a baby. They gave birth to babies who were often extremely irritable and had many gastrointestinal troubles. In the second intermediate group, the mothers were uneasy about being pregnant. But there again, Rottman's psychological tests and the babies themselves revealed something else. These apparently rejecting mothers unconsciously wanted their babies. Not surprisingly, the babies were physically healthy, happy, and secure.

The overriding goal of Month Two is to resolve all your emotional trouble spots as completely as possible. Indeed, strong emotional conflict might cause you to neglect your diet, to drink or smoke, or as the pregnancy goes on, to avoid prenatal classes ("because all the other couples seem to get along so well"). Psychological strain will also saddle you with an extra burden of worry, causing you to flood your unborn child with stress hormones. On the other hand, a happy and relaxed attitude can go a long way toward making your baby feel wanted and loved.

Though you will learn a number of new techniques during Month Two of your pregnancy, you should continue to carry out the core techniques you mastered during Month One. As in your first month, a primary goal of Month Two is heightened self-confidence and relaxation. This can be best achieved by listening to music and practicing alert progressive relaxation. Stay deeply attuned to your inner emotions through daily journal writing and dream work. Keeping up with these basic techniques will make it easier for you to absorb the new exercises presented here.

Exercise 6: Feast on a Star

THEME: Invigorating your body
INSTRUMENT: Visualization
PARTICIPANT: Mother
TEMPO: At least once a day, whenever you feel tired

The exhaustion you may feel during your second month of pregnancy is giving you a clear signal to rest. Whenever you feel especially tired, you should sit in a comfortable chair with your feet up, close your eyes, and relax. If you are able to take a short nap during periods of extreme exhaustion, do so.

But if you are like many people, you may not be able to spend large parts of your day lying around. You may have a job or small, active children. Or you may simply want to boost your energy level so that you can enjoy a friend, a book, a good meal, or any pleasant part of your life. Therefore, after you have taken a sufficient rest, you might increase your energy with a visualization technique that was developed for athletes. Athletes who call on high levels of energy for activities such as sprinting or jumping must be prepared mentally as well as physically. They have to find a special, almost superhuman power within themselves at the precise moment of competition when performance counts. The same ability, sports psychologists contend, might help writers compose dialogue, actors perfect their characters, and business people negotiate deals. Visualization can also help pregnant women feel refreshed and revitalized, ready to carry on with their day.

Remember, you can do this exercise virtually anywhere, anytime of the night or day. You may "Feast on a Star" on a bus on the way to work, in the shower, or even while cooking dinner for your family.

To achieve an energy boost, think of something that makes you feel invigorated—it can be a sight, a feeling, or a sound. Before she went out on the ice, for instance, one professional skater always imagined swallowing a star and having it burst inside her, spreading energy from the tips of her fingers to her toes. A runner imagined a rubber band of light propelling him from the start of the race to the end. Carefully choose the image that's right for you. We suggest that you seek gentler images than those conjured by athletes involved in highly competitive endeavors. You might envision the blinking green cursor of your word processor zipping through your body or the brisk, cool flow of a spring breeze; the refreshing spray of a lawn sprinkler; or the image of waves along the shore.

Once you have chosen the energizing image that best suits you, think about it and develop it so that it is truly brimming with vitality. Use all your senses to create or recreate the scene so that it is as vivid as you can make it.

Any time you feel especially tired and would like a boost, picture this special image. After a while, the image will automatically stimulate your nervous system to respond with a surge of physical well-being.

By the way, you can use similar visualization techniques to help you deal with nausea. Images that may help you keep your nausea under control include an inner sprinkler system to cool your body and wash away the feelings of sickness; a soothing but brisk "mint" gel coating your stomach and digestive tract; a light, white, cool inner snow.

You can also reduce that nauseous feeling by sipping soda or munching on crackers. Be careful about eating *too* much, however. Consuming excessively starchy or sugary food and drink to alleviate nausea may lead to unwanted weight gain. If you feel you must have something to put in your mouth frequently, we suggest celery sticks and orange or cherry flavored seltzer (without the sugar).

Exercise 7: Hello, Baby

THEME: Communicating warmth and security to the unborn
INSTRUMENT: Affirmations
PARTICIPANTS: Mother and unborn child
TEMPO: Ten to twenty minutes, once or twice a week for the duration of your pregnancy

Even though your baby is only half an inch long and weighs less than an aspirin tablet, this is a good time to start telling her she is wanted and loved. Using the affirmation technique described here, start to communicate with your unborn.

Scan the list below and choose the affirmation or affirmations that seem best suited to you. If you prefer, create an affirmation of your own. After you have an appropriate statement in mind, simply repeat it to yourself ten to twenty times whenever you want to communicate your love and support to the child within.

You need not respond to these affirmations with negative reactions on a sheet of paper. If negative reactions emerge spontaneously, however, you might want to deal with them in writing using the instructions presented for Exercise 4.

- *All the cells, tissues, and organs in your body are now developing perfectly.*
- *You are loved and wanted.*
- *I love feeling you grow inside me.*
- *You are warm, secure, and happy.*
- *You are my baby and I want you more than anything in the world.*

Exercise 8: The Right-Brain Spin

THEME: Expressing your deepest thoughts and feelings
INSTRUMENT: Journal
PARTICIPANT: Mother
TEMPO: At least forty minutes, whenever you have trouble getting at your true feelings

As you progress through the Womb Harmonics program, continue to express your deepest feelings and thoughts through writing. Especially in the next few exercises, you will use your journal to help you delve into your most essential self. To aid this process, we introduce a four-part writing technique for tapping the right hemisphere of the brain, the seat of intuition and spontaneous thought. Drawn in part from the work of psychologist Henriette Anne Klauser, an expert on writing blocks, the technique we suggest will free you up so that you can put your deepest emotions spontaneously onto the page.

Indeed, when it is free to express itself, the emotional, highly intuitive right hemisphere will reveal a wellspring of hidden truth. The problem is that the free-wheeling style of the right hemisphere is often repressed by the cautious, analytical left hemisphere. By following the four-step system below, you will be able to keep your left brain at bay while your right brain spins out a revealing array of images and thoughts. Then, after you have expressed yourself as honestly as possible, your left hemisphere can enter the scene, analyzing and making sense of the words you have spontaneously put on the page.

To tap the energy and flow of your right brain, sit down to write in your journal just as you always do. But instead of carefully formulating your words, write whatever comes into your mind, no matter how nonsensical it might seem. In fact, if you feel your writing is boring or silly, say so right on the page. The important thing is to keep writing as fluidly as possible without letting up—even if you feel like stopping—for at least ten minutes. This time frame is especially important to keep in mind if you hit what professional writers sometimes call "the wall"—a point at which you feel you are unbearably boring or have nothing more to say. If you reach the wall before your time limit is up, keep writing no matter what. Continue to express your feelings—including the fact that you believe what you are writing is boring—and you may soon find that you have written your way through *the wall to some startling inner truths. Using this technique, you may discover your deepest feelings about events in your past—and in your present and future.*

After the ten-minute period is up, take another ten to fifteen minutes to reflect. This period of reflection should take place away from the spot you occupied while writing. Wher-

ever you go, make sure you have your journal with you. Before your period of reflection actually begins, say to yourself, If I am to tap into my deepest feelings through journal writing, I must allow my deepest thoughts to spontaneously flow.

After your period of reflection is up, stop and spend another ten minutes writing in your journal. Remember to keep writing even if you hit a "wall."

Finally, as the last step in this exercise, we would like you to express the ideas and feelings you have been trying to get at through an unconventional writing technique called "branching." While most journal writing takes place in a somewhat sequential fashion, with one thought following the next from beginning to end, branching starts in the middle and allows you to work your way out in all directions via a radiating "branching chart."

To make your own branching chart, start by drawing a circle in the middle of a page. Like the trunk of a tree, this circle should contain the central idea or feeling you are trying to express. After you have drawn your circle and printed your goal or theme within, spend ten minutes drawing and labeling branches radiating from the center. Each main branch should represent a thought or idea directly related to the central trunk. Smaller branches, stemming out from larger ones, should represent refinements, modifications, or additions to the major branches. Each sub-branch should be labeled as well. As you continue to draw and label branches, turn your paper, inserting new ideas whenever they occur to you.

Because the branching technique is by nature associative, it gives your free-wheeling right brain the chance to emerge. It can reveal thought patterns, priorities, and preferences of which you were previously unaware; often, the technique gives vent to feelings that have simply been ignored. For instance,

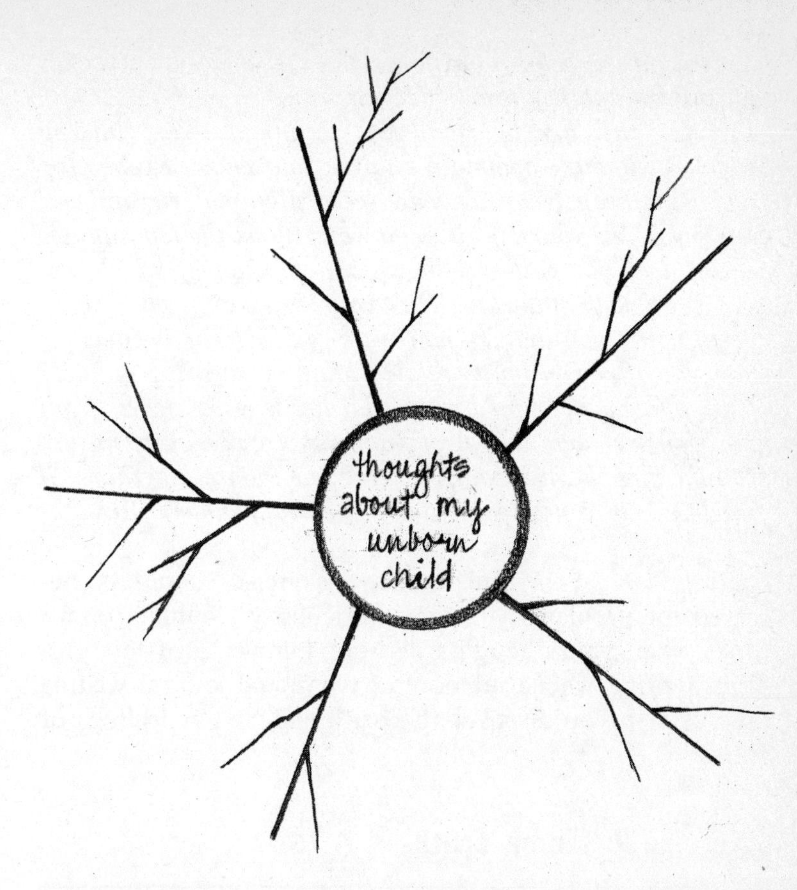

you may discover you fear the expected pain of childbirth, or interference from your mother once your baby is born. You may discover an undercurrent of guilt about your intention to stay at your job—or you may find you resent leaving work after your baby is born. Branching can also reveal feelings usually left out of journal entries because they don't seem to fit the writer's notion of what is proper—feelings that seem embarrassing or absurd. Do you fear your unborn child will be ugly, or that you will drop her after she is born? Often, these seemingly silly or extreme feelings are the very ones that provide the key to our deepest fears.

To get full benefit from this technique, keep adding branches without stopping to analyze your chart. Keep going even if the branches you create seem silly or irrelevant and even if you feel yourself hitting a wall. When the ten minutes are up, look for patterns, ideas, and feelings of which you were previously unaware. Has your branching chart connected issues you didn't know were related? For instance, is your fear of responsibility related to an overbearing mother? Does your chart reveal any special anxieties or fears, from fear of miscarriage to fear of financial stress? Consistent use of branching charts throughout the nine-month program will probably help you discover some important inner truths.

Special Note: This time-intensive exercise should be reserved for problems you find particularly troubling or for times when your thoughts just don't flow. Turn to right-brain writing whenever more conventional journal writing fails to help you discover the truth about your feelings or fears.

Exercise 9: Home Truths

THEME: Exploring your childhood home
INSTRUMENT: Journal
PARTICIPANT: Mother
TEMPO: Forty minutes, once this month

In this exercise, you will travel down the hallway of your mind to the place you spent the first six years of your life. This may be a house, an apartment, a farm, or any other structure or locale. If you moved one or more times during this period, pick the place you remember best. By remembering your past, you will find it easier to tune into your deepest feelings. If negative, these feelings should be resolved to help you be the best parent you can be. If positive, these feelings will help you empathize with the needs of the child within you.

After you have spent about five minutes recalling your childhood home, take out your journal and carry out steps 1 through 5.

1. List each room in the house you have recalled. Start with the room you remember best.

2. Draw a floor plan of your old home. Include staircases, windows, furniture, plants, and as much other detail as you can.

3. Go back to your old home in your mind, and with the help of the floor plan, slowly walk through it. Using all your senses, try to experience your childhood home as fully as possible. What color is the couch? What texture is the fabric covering the chair? What do you smell in the kitchen? In your bedroom? In the den? What is your favorite spot? Are there pictures, posters, calendars, or clocks on the walls? Where did you hide your most treasured possessions?

4. Explore your emotional memories of your home by asking yourself these questions:

What was I not allowed to touch?

Where was I not allowed to go?

Do I remember crying in one of the rooms? What exactly happened?

Do I remember laughing really hard in one of the rooms? What exactly happened?

Do I remember being very angry in one of the rooms? What exactly happened?

Do I remember feeling very close to my mother or father in one of these rooms?

Do I remember overhearing something I shouldn't have in one of these rooms?

5. Now go to the window of the room you slept in. Look out. What do you see? Take your time. Look at the ground and the house or building across the street. Look to the right and to the left. See the seasons changing. Do you see snow on your windowsill? If so, what do you do with it? Continue to remember the time you spent at this window. Has anything seen from this window left a lasting impression on you? If so, describe the scene in as much detail as possible.

Exercise 10: Snapshots

THEME: Exploring your relationship to your parents
INSTRUMENT: Journal and photographs (or photolike memories)
PARTICIPANT: Mother
TEMPO: Sixty minutes, once this month

In this exercise you will continue to journey back into your childhood. But this time the focus will be your relationship with your parents and siblings, if any. Old family photos (or your memory of them) will be your ticket to the past. As in the previous exercise, remembering and resolving past conflicts will ease your mind, enabling you to direct more love and acceptance at the child about to be born. Remembering happy childhood events will increase your enthusiasm and empathy for your baby and help reinforce your bonds with the folks who offer you support and love.

If you have a photo album or some loose photographs of yourself as a child, get them now. The photos you dig up should include as many members of your immediate family as possible. If you have no access to old photographs, take a few minutes to consider what photos of your childhood family would *look like if you could have them in front of you. Do not worry about whether your memories capture the real photographs exactly. Your inner impressions, accurate or not, will be sufficient to help you through the four steps of this exercise.*

1. As you look through your old family photographs—or recall your impressions *of them—answer as many of the following questions as you can:*

- *Are there any recurrent patterns or themes? For instance, do you always stand closest to one parent? If so, what does this say to you about your relationship to this parent and the other parent?*
- *Is someone always absent from the pictures? If so, is this because that person is taking all the pictures? What does this tell you about the missing individual and the others?*
- *Are there subgroups within the pictures? For instance, do you and your sister always stand together? Do your mother and father always stand together? Or does your mother always stand a few inches apart, holding the baby?*
- *Do people stand without touching, frozen in solitude, or do you see a lot of closeness and touching?*
- *Read the body language in the photos. Family members may be standing or sitting close together, but their heads may be inclined toward someone or tilted away from someone else. As you study the pictures, do you see the expression of an underlying feeling or prevalent mood?*
- *Look very closely at the faces—and especially the eyes and the mouths—of family members in the photos. Is there a discrepancy between these separate features? For instance, is the mouth smiling while the eyes look suspicious or fearful?*
- *Are you and others dressed in an appropriate fashion for*

the photos you are studying? Is the dress frequently casual or formal?

- *Who is the center of attention in the photos?*
- *Do you notice a gradual or sudden weight gain or loss in any family member as you study photos taken over a period of time? Are any other significant changes apparent? If so, what does the change mean?*
- *Look at a picture of your mother or father engaged in an activity like painting or gardening. What is the importance of that activity to their personality—and to you today?*
- *Describe the expression on each person's face. If you had to choose an animal to define each person in the picture, which animals would you choose?*

2. In your mind's eye, compose an ideal family picture based on a scene from any part of your childhood. You might envision a birthday celebration, a Thanksgiving dinner, or a lazy summer day by the pool. If no scene immediately comes to mind, invent one. Use words, arrows, stick figures, and whatever else will help you to draw an accurate picture. When you are finished, write down your thoughts and feelings.

3. Draw a portrait of your mother and your father in their most characteristic pose, wearing the clothes and holding the objects or pets you most closely associate with them. You may create full-blown, anatomically correct figures or stick figures, and you may explain your drawing with words, arrows, or whatever else will make your picture emotionally accurate. When you are finished, write down your thoughts and feelings.

4. Find one snapshot of your parents fighting and one in which they are really close and loving. If no such photos exist, imagine them in your mind's eye. Consider the implications of these photos. If you do not remember your parents ever fighting or embracing, consider the implication of that. Then picture them engaged in these activities now.

After you have completed the four steps above, reflect on what you have learned. If you have uncovered painful memories, tell yourself you need not repeat these experiences in your *family. Then let these memories go. If you have uncovered positive aspects of your past, reflect on how you may incorporate these elements into your life now.*

Exercise 11: The Pregnant Pause

THEME: Your feelings about pregnancy
INSTRUMENTS: Journal and affirmations
PARTICIPANT: Mother
TEMPO: A couple of times a week, then until any negative feelings you may have are resolved

Today we know for certain that the unborn child's physical and mental growth is affected not only by what her mother eats, drinks and inhales, but also by what she experiences, feels and thinks. Deeply felt positive thoughts, we now know, can induce a sense of calm in an unborn child.

Negative or displeasing thoughts, on the other hand, may induce chemical or neurological changes in your body and quickly send the message to baby as well. Since it is the rare pregnancy that procedes idyllically from beginning to end, even the happiest mothers may experience some doubts. You might worry about your adequacy as a parent, for instance, or about the added financial responsibilities parenthood will entail. You may worry about miscarriage or fear for the health of the unborn child. Often, pregnancy comes as a surprise. In such instances, you may feel unprepared for a child, or fear that a new baby will complicate your life.

These negative feelings are natural. That said, remember that your unborn child needs your love and acceptance. To get to the point where you can infuse your baby with largely positive feelings, you must come to terms with your negative impulses.

To get to the root of your doubts about your pregnancy, your relationship with your husband or anything else, find a free period of time to answer the questions below. Enter the questions in your journal, then respond to them without much thought or analysis. You need not answer the questions in order or even in one sitting. But deal with all these questions this month. You may make your answers as long and detailed as you like. And remember—be completely honest.

- *Do I want to be pregnant now?*
- *Is this a good time for me to have a baby?*
- *How does my partner feel about my being pregnant?*
- *How does my partner feel about having a child?*
- *How will my mother and father feel about my being pregnant?*
- *How will I cope emotionally?*
- *How will I cope financially?*
- *How will my baby affect my career?*
- *How will my baby affect my relationship with my partner?*
- *How will my baby affect my relationship with my other children (if any)?*

After you have answered all the questions, use conventional journal writing or the right-brain-writing technique previously presented to further explore your feelings.

Continue to address the issues elicited by this exercise until you believe all doubts related to your pregnancy have been brought to the surface. In most instances, this technique should help you come to terms with these doubts, allowing a more positive outlook to emerge. If you continue to worry about any aspect of pregnancy, childbirth, or parenthood, we urge you to consult your obstetrician or perhaps even a psychotherapist or counselor.

Month Two Summary

New Techniques

6. Feast on a Star	Energy booster	Once a day, when needed
7. Hello, Baby	Communicating with the unborn baby	10–20 minutes, twice weekly
8. The Right-Brain Spin	Writing	40 minutes, when needed
9. Home Truths	Examining your childhood	40 minutes
10. Snapshots	Exploring the family you grew up with	60 minutes
11. The Pregnant Pause	Exploring your feelings about pregnancy	Whenever needed

Familiar Techniques to Continue

1. Viva Vivaldi	Music to grow by	60 minutes, twice weekly
2. Time Out for Mom	Relaxation	20 minutes, once a day
3. Daily Diary	Writing	Every day, as needed
4. Affirmations	Positive thinking	At least 2 minutes, twice daily

5. Dream Work	Understanding dreams	Every time you have a dream

Your Baby at Two Months' Gestation

WEEK	DAY	SIZE AND WEIGHT	EMBRYOLOGICAL AND FUNCTIONAL CHANGES
5	35	.33 in. (8 mm) .001 oz (2.8 mgm)	The three primary parts of the brain are present, along with all cranial and spinal nerves. Eyes, ears, and nose are starting to form. Eyes have pigment and outer ears have auditory canals. Arm buds and leg buds prominent. Heart cavity develops chambers. Digestive tract, spleen, and pancreas are formed. The umbilical cord is fully established.
6	42	.5 in. (13 mm)	The arms are too short to meet, but the rudiments of fingers and toes appear. The tip of the nose has formed. Some major brain centers, including the thalamus, hypothalamus, and cerebellum are established. The head and neck make up half the body. Cartilage and bones develop, testes and ovaries appear. Reflexes such as sucking and grasping begin. The heart pumps blood, and the fetal electrocardiogram is similar to that of adults. The embryo responds to touch, and strong, brisk movements appear.
7		.8 in. (2 cm) 0.07 oz (2 gm)	From this point on, the developing child ceases to be an embryo and

		becomes a fetus. The face rounds out and begins to look human. A distinct neck connects the head with the body. Other developments: the semicircular canals of the ear, the palate of the mouth, the heart valves and the nerve cells of the retina form. The baby responds to tactile stimulation.
8	2.25 in. (4 cm) 0.10 oz (3 gm) Diameter of a half-dollar, lighter than a Valium tablet	The eyes move to the front of the face. Taste buds form. The head comprises half the body. The stomach is big, while the arms and legs are small. Light stroking of the upper lip or nostrils will cause the head and trunk to bend. Brain-wave activity now resembles that of human adults.

You at Two Months of Pregnancy

WEEK	THE PREGNANCY EXPERIENCE
5	Classic pregnancy symptoms may begin. You may start to urinate frequently, and veins may become more prominent. You may start to have morning sickness, including nausea. You probably feel more tired than usual; for some, the exhaustion is extreme. Your breasts may enlarge and become tender or even hurt. The pigmented area around your nipples, known as the areola, should darken, and milk ducts may start to form. Your breasts may show evidence of stretch marks. Your gums may soften or even bleed.
6–7	Your uterus becomes enlarged, and your cervix becomes soft and bluish. Physical diagnosis of the pregnancy is now possible. A fluid known as colostrum may be expressed from your breasts. Nausea and exhaustion may increase.
8	You may notice your waist thickening and may have trouble wearing your most fitted clothing.

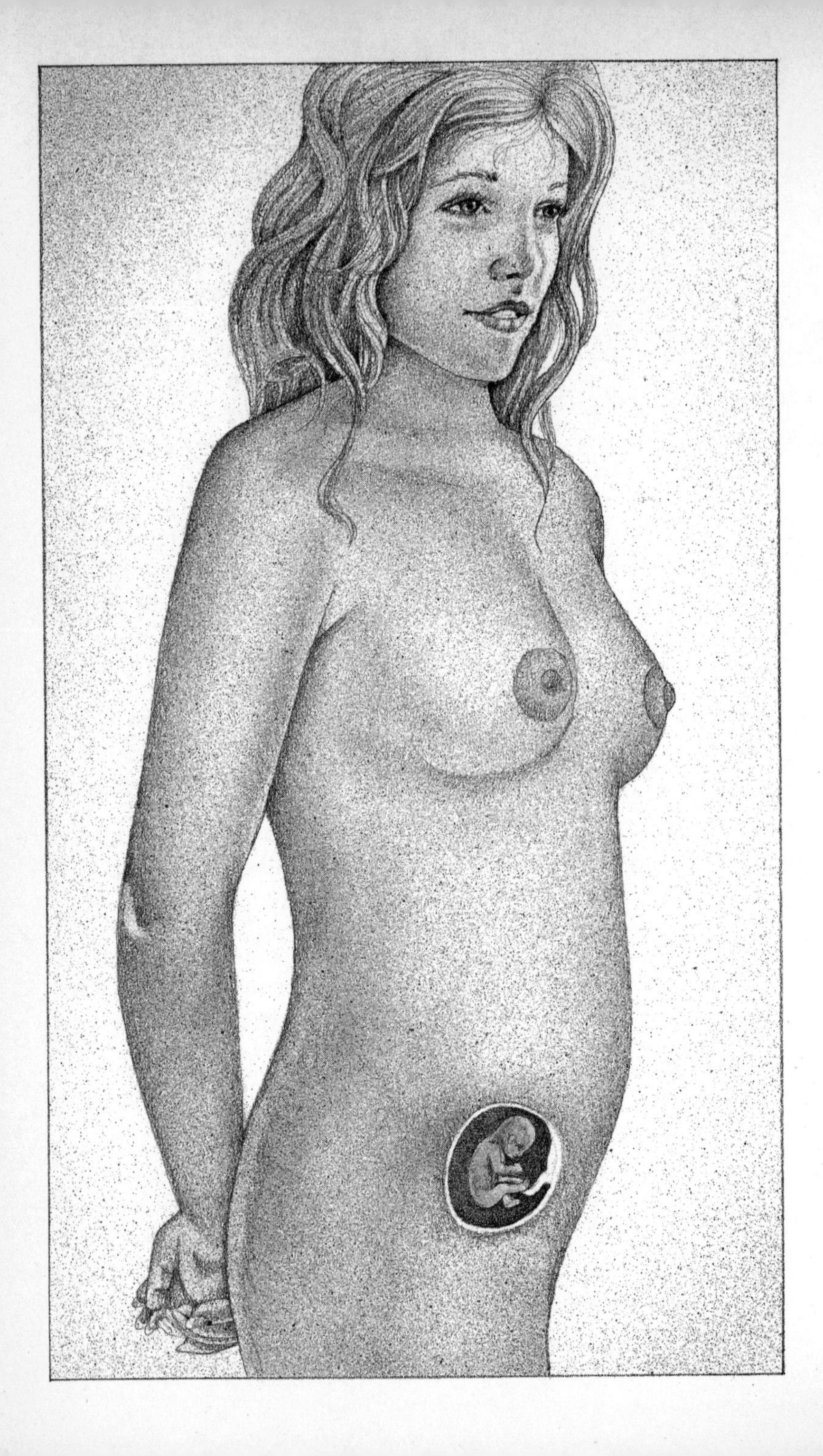

3

MONTH THREE: Growing Together

One of the most striking and dramatic events you've probably ever experienced was that of your own birth. For nine months you floated gently in the warm, dark, watery universe of your mother's womb. Every so often, a muffled sound or strong maternal emotion intruded upon your tranquil world, but for the most part, you were at one with your peaceful environment. Then one day, virtually without warning, you felt a powerful jolt, and the soothing swirls and eddies of the amniotic sea gave way to contractions of seismic force. Your journey through the birth canal had begun.

Your tortuous odyssey ended hours later, when your head poked through the vaginal opening. If your birth was ideal, classical music played in the background and you got to suckle your mother's breast as your father stood nearby. If you had a routine medical birth, you found yourself in a bright, cold, noisy, bustling room. Strangers probed and examined you while your mother, languishing on a table, waited to get a peek.

For most of this century, medical experts believed that newborns were immune to the conditions of their birth. In fact, the notion that the birth experience had any lasting impact at all was considered absurd. But today, extraordinary new research leaves little doubt that the experience of birth has a profound effect on us all.

Writing in the prestigious medical journal *Lancet,* for instance, the well-known psychologist Lee Salk of Cornell University Medical School has attributed some teenage suicide to the trauma of a difficult delivery. In fact, he found that suicide victims in his study generally lacked early prenatal care, had mothers who were chronically ill during pregnancy, and suffered respiratory distress for more than an hour after birth. In a related study, Dr. Bertil Jacobson of Stockholm's Karolinska Institute discovered that adult drug addiction is often related to birth trauma. With disturbing frequency, drug addicts were born in hospitals where doctors most often administered opiates, barbiturates, or chloroform to women in labor. These drugs passed through the umbilical cord to the child, Jacobson suggests, making him more susceptible to drug addiction later in life. (Today, of course, women who study Lamaze and practice natural childbirth can avoid drugs completely while giving birth. They can also avoid those hospitals that routinely administer drugs.)

Research suggests that birth style may influence personality in other ways as well. In a study conducted by social worker Dennis McCracken, for instance, sixty cesarean children who did not experience labor were compared to sixty vaginally born children who did experience labor. McCracken, who reported his findings at a recent conference sponsored by PPPANA, found that the cesarean children seemed more intuitive and open to experience, while the vaginally born children seemed more conscientious and confident. Following this report, physician Lewis Bissell suggested that the increasingly large number of cesarean-born children could lead to an alteration in social attitudes throughout the world.

We caution you to put these findings, many of them still preliminary in perspective. Try to avoid using drugs during childbirth, of course, and aim for a natural, healthy delivery. However, do not worry if your baby's birth was a difficult one. Even children who have had extremely traumatic births will thrive if their parents are loving and supportive *after* they are born.

For most individuals, birth, be it idyllic or traumatic, cesarean or breech, is shrouded in mystery, masked by sheer failure of memory and the veil of time. Some psychologists, however, believe it is possible to recall that distant event down to the color of our mother's gown and the meaning of the doctor's remarks.

One of the first people to uncover what seemed like bona-fide birth memories was California obstetrician David B. Cheek. In one of his most impressive studies, Cheek showed that people retain a muscle memory of the way their heads, shoulders, and arms moved as they entered the world. "As an obstetrician," Cheek explained to us, "I knew that when a baby comes out the birth canal, it automatically rotates its head in a particular fashion. I also noticed that whenever I asked my patients about birth, they spontaneously turned their heads in a similar way. So I got the idea that maybe they were remembering the same physiological mechanism they'd experienced while being born."

To validate this theory, Cheek recruited some patients he had delivered decades before. He hypnotized these individuals, then asked them to recall their births. His plan: to compare each report to the original birth record. To Cheek's surprise, each patient correctly remembered the direction in which his or her head had rotated upon leaving the birth canal. Virtually all Cheek's patients correctly reported which of their arms came out first as well.

Finally, in one of the most fascinating studies to emerge

from the field of pre- and perinatal psychology, San Diego psychologist David B. Chamberlain has collected what he believes are accurate memories of birth. Chamberlain was intrigued after hearing one of his clients report what seemed like a highly specific birth memory. To investigate further, he asked ten mother-offspring pairs to participate in his study. After regressing each subject under hypnosis, Chamberlain asked a battery of questions related to birth events. Mothers and children alike told him startlingly similar details of the offspring's birth. One daughter, for instance, correctly described her mother's hairstyle at the time of her birth. Another accurately recalled her mother smelling her, then expressing concern over the normality of her toes. And another described precisely a debate between her mother and father over her name.

Still other researchers report a plethora of birth memories pouring forth from the very young. Linda Mathison of Seattle has discovered that young children, either spontaneously or in response to direct questions, frequently come up with detailed memories of birth. Most of these reports, Mathison has found, emerge between the ages of two-and-a-half and three-and-a-half.

One of the most spectacular reports comes from New York psychiatrist Rima Laibow. Laibow was giving her young son a bath, she remembers, when he looked up at her and said, "I have some questions about when I was new."

"What do you mean?" Laibow asked.

"When I was brand new," he replied. And then his questions began.

"He wanted to know where the bottom half of everyone's face was," Laibow recalls, "and why there was a bright light over his head, and what the funny noise was."

In fact, Laibow says, all these things had occurred. Doctors and nurses were wearing surgical masks, the noise came from suction equipment, and surgical lights were glaring for all to see.

As fascinating as such stories may be, of course, extraordinary theories require extraordinary levels of proof. And it goes without saying that anecdotal reports of detailed birth memories must be backed up by scientifically controlled studies before we can accept them as valid. Some researchers, for instance, believe these memories represent our fantasies of the way our earliest lives must have been. In these images, they see emotionally valid metaphors for our entry to the world, not literal transcripts of events. Other experts point out that some of the data are problematic because they are derived by means of hypnosis. Hypnosis, the experts explain, may induce "pseudomemories" that take the place of real ones; that is why information derived from hypnosis is not valid in a court of law.

But even if we don't observe our births in Dolby sound and Technicolor, solid research shows that the birth experience deeply affects us all. Perhaps, as Bertil Jacobson proposes, birth results in a type of "imprinting," a learning mechanism by which social attachments and self-identity are established rapidly, very early on. (Imprinting is a crucial process in chickens and many other species, but it has never been proven to exist in human beings.) Or perhaps our earliest experience seems so predictive because it leads naturally to the world we encounter as we grow.

In light of the best available scientific evidence, we provide a series of exercises aimed at helping you explore your birth experience. Using these techniques, you may be able to get in touch with memories or feelings you have long forgotten; you may even be able to change present behavior patterns established when you were born. At the very least, you will arrive at a deeper understanding of how the *adult* you feels and thinks about your birth. Regardless of whether the images the exercises evoke are rooted in absolute fact, they should enhance your insight into your own infancy and childhood. They should also make it easier for you, as a prospective mother, to empathize with your unborn child and to prepare for the upcoming experience of labor and birth.

Before you actually begin the exercises, you may want to use the drawing technique for accessing your intuitive right brain and tapping your subconscious mind. This technique (Exercise 12, "Right-Brain Doodles"), along with the right-brain writing introduced during Month Two, can help you sort out your impressions about birth.

Our first birth-memory exercise ("The Seed," Exercise 13), is geared to help you recapture the "feeling" of the womb. It relies on a technique known as guided imagery. Using this technique, you will imagine yourself in the form of a seed growing into a full-size flower or tree. Other birth memory exercises include Exercise 14, "Back to the Womb," in which pictures of embryonic development help to trigger birth-related images and sensations, and Exercise 15, "The Amniotic Sea," in which you will attempt to experience womb sensations by taking a warm bath with the lights out.

The final exercise, "The Inner Circle," features mandala drawing. This ancient psychological technique, in which you draw meaningful pictures inside circles, should help you clarify your feelings and sustain a balanced point of view.

Please remember to continue the core techniques you mastered during Months One and Two. Even though you are exploring your impressions of the distant past, it is vitally important that you remain relaxed and that you stay in touch with your emotions. Continue to explore your childhood through conventional and right-brain writing techniques. You will find that the more you stay in touch with your feelings, the calmer and happier you and your unborn child will become.

Exercise 12: Right-Brain Doodles

THEME: Tuning into the right brain
INSTRUMENTS: Lead pencil, paper or journal, cassette tape, and this book
PARTICIPANTS: Mother and father
TEMPO: Thirty–forty minutes, whenever you wish to access your intuitive self

As you already know, the right hemisphere of your brain is associated with spontaneity and intuition. To tap your innermost unconscious feelings—to learn how you feel about a whole range of issues, including relationships or pregnancy—it is often necessary to give this hemisphere greater freedom of expression. Toward this end, you mastered a potent technique for right-brain journal writing in Month Two. But since the right hemisphere is so intrinsically *visual,* a technique for right-brain drawing is appropriate. By literally "tuning up" the right hemisphere of your brain as your left hemisphere is "tuned down," you will be able to create artistic impressions of your deepest desires and fears.

This three-step exercise has been adapted from California State University (Long Beach) art professor Betty Edwards. The goal is to enhance your communication with your right hemisphere, giving you a clearer notion of the wisdom and insight contained within.

The first step in right-brain doodling simply quiets the

chatter of your left brain so your right brain can be heard. Before you start this exercise, make sure that you have four things by your side: your journal or paper, a lead pencil, a cassette tape and player, and this book. Read the instructions through before you begin. After all, since right-brain doodling is a distinctly *nonverbal* task, reading instructions as you proceed might get in the way.

Step One

After you have gathered your materials and read the instructions, please play the Viva Vivaldi tape (including the alert progressive relaxation induction and musical selection) you created during Month One. When you have finished listening to the entire tape, you will be in a state of alert relaxation.

Now take your journal and pencil in hand. Turn to page 50 of this book, where you will see a picture of the unborn child at three months' gestation. Turn the picture upside-down and begin to copy it—also upside-down—into your journal. Start your drawing at the top and work your way down. Do not try to recognize or give names to specific body parts; instead, pay attention to the lines and angles, the areas of shadow and the areas of light.

The act of drawing upside-down, Edwards explains, suppresses the left brain and helps the right brain come to the fore. The reason: Upside-down images cause recognition problems for the analytic, literal-minded left brain; the visual right brain, however, easily grasps the relationship between lines, angles, and shapes.

After you have finished this part of the exercise and turned your upside-down drawing right-side up, you will probably find that your version is surprisingly precise. Your artistic creation will, most probably, be far more skillful than you had hoped. But more important, the act of drawing upside-down will have helped you make a cognitive shift so that, for a while at least, your right brain holds sway.

If you have followed our instructions, you will find that your right hemisphere has been primed. In its dominant, expressive mode, it can help you get in touch with sensations such as peacefulness, anger, depression, and joy. It can also reveal your true feelings about people and situations in your past and present life.

After your right brain has been primed in Step One, you may want to get more deeply in touch with your feelings toward pregnancy, motherhood, your spouse, or any other pressing issue through the related drawing technique in Step Two.

Step Two

This time, consider an issue that you find particularly compelling. This is a good time, for instance, to work on some of the issues that surfaced during Month Two. Are you concerned about a past event in your childhood? Your status on the job once your baby is born? Your relationship with your mother? The upcoming labor and birth? Whatever topic you choose, think about it for a few minutes. As you consider the subject matter, however, do not define it in words. Instead, try to visualize *the problem by letting pictures run through your mind. They may consist of clear images of actual persons or scenes; colors or patterns of light; or just a word or idea. Stay with the image you have created for at least ten minutes. Be patient. The right brain does not like to be rushed.*

After you have finished this visualization process, take your journal and turn to a blank page. Using your pencil, draw a border or frame. Working within the border, draw the image —and the associated emotions—conjured just before. As you draw, avoid any literal pictures or symbols. *If you are concerned about your mother, for instance, do not draw a woman or a heart. Do not create rainbows, starbursts, or eyes.*

Instead, use the point or side of your pencil lead to create lines and marks. *You may create wide or narrow marks; use heavy or light pressure; generate lines that are straight or curved, short or long. Feel free to fill in all the space within your border or just a tiny fraction of it. The best way to produce your right-brain doodle is simply to immerse yourself in the* emotion *created by the situation you are trying to resolve. Visualize the emotion flowing from within your body through your fingertips to the pencil and onto the page. Create as many right-brain doodles as you like. When you feel you have expressed yourself sufficiently, put your pencil down.*

After a few minutes, study your drawings. They may help you see your concerns from a different point of view. Hold your doodle (or doodles) at arm's length and study it. You are looking at a message from the intuitive part of your brain. What does it say? Which part of the drawing represents you? Which lines and curves represent the important people in your life or the world at large? By studying your creation, can you see your unborn child or your partner? Have you created a joyful, enthusiastic picture? A sensual one? Or do your lines and curves communicate anxiety and fear?

For instance, one woman had been angry at her overcritical mother for years. After studying her doodles—strong, raylike arms reaching out in all directions from a central sphere—she glimpsed a connection between her mother and herself. She realized that her mother *had* truly loved her, and that she could provide the *positive* aspects of her own upbringing to the child within her.

After you have studied your doodles for a while, it may be helpful to state their message in words. Here's how.

Step Three

As you study your doodles, consider the words that best communicate their meaning. Look at each doodle separately, state the words that best define it aloud, then write the words next to each drawing. Now shut your eyes and hold the words and pictures in your mind at once.

To see messages that might remain hidden or obscure, turn your doodle upside-down. Do any new elements pop out? If so, define these new features in words. Write the words down again. Then shut your eyes and hold the words and pictures in your mind at once.

Right-brain doodles may give you a whole new way of seeing things. If you can glimpse a confusing issue from an alternate point of view, a resolution may emerge.

Exercise 13—The Seed

THEME: Exploring your own prenatal and birth experience
INSTRUMENTS: Guided imagery, cassette tape, paper and crayons
PARTICIPANTS: Mother and father
TEMPO: Sixty minutes

This exercise takes you on a very gentle and pleasant journey through your mind. You may experience anything from a sense of relaxation and bliss to a flood of feelings and perhaps even memories about your own womb life and birth. But try to avoid unrealistic expectations. Accept whatever insights your particular experience happens to reveal. Repeating this exercise may well provide you with additional insights into your own experience of pregnancy and birth.

We suggest that you and your partner perform this exercise together. If you attend a prenatal class, you may wish to share this exercise with couples there as well. The greater the number of people you have participating in this extraordinary journey, the more exciting it becomes.

Remember, proceed with this exercise only when you have plenty of time to enjoy it. You should practice "The Seed" at least once, but you may repeat it as often as you like.

To perform this exercise, please have a close friend read the instructions into a tape recorder. (Note that "The Seed" begins the same way as "Time Out for Mom," the alert relaxation exercise you learned during Month One.) After you have become sufficiently relaxed, the guided imagery part of this exercise can begin. Follow the guided-imagery segment of this exercise with ten minutes of Baroque music added on to the end of the tape. (You may use the music suggested in Exercise 1, "Viva Vivaldi.")

> *The script for the tape reads as follows:*
>
> *Close your eyes and take a couple of* deep breaths. *Continue to breathe* deeply *and* evenly, *allowing yourself to focus on the rhythm of your breathing, on your bodily sensations, and on any feelings and images about yourself. If thoughts about the outside world intrude upon you, just let them pass the way clouds pass over the horizon. Notice them, and then let them go.*

Now I would like you to become aware of your feet. *How do they feel pressed against the footstool? Notice the pressure on them, and the angle at which they are placed. Become aware of the* soles of your feet. *Notice your heels, your toes, your ankles. Now begin to curl your toes toward the soles of your feet, as if trying to touch them. Push your toes* down, down, down. Hold *them and then let go.*

Breathe *in and out. Now relax and let go.*

With each breath *that you take, you are* choosing *to go* deeper *and* deeper *into a perfect state of relaxation. You are not falling asleep. You remain alert but relaxed.*

Now become aware of your legs, *from your* knees *down to your* ankles. *As you become aware of your legs, I want you to* tighten *all your leg muscles. Tighten, tighten, tighten.* Hold. *And relax.*

Breathe *in and out. Now relax and let go.*

With each breath that you take you are going deeper and deeper *into yourself, and your body is becoming* more and more *relaxed.*

Now focus your attention on the middle of your body—your thighs, *your* pelvis, *and your* buttocks. *As you become aware, tighten all the muscles in these areas.* Tighten, tighten, tighten. Hold. *And* relax.

Breathe *in and out. Now relax and let go.*

Continue to breathe deeply *and* evenly. *With each inhalation, you are breathing in fresh oxygen and fresh energy. With each exhalation, you are breathing out carbon dioxide and bodily wastes. Think of each* inhalation *as a way of taking in love and support from the universe. Think of each* exhalation *as a means of ejecting negative feelings and tension.*

Now go on to the next section of your body. Become aware of your spine *from your pelvis to the base of your head. Begin to* press *against the back of your chair or supporting cushions along the length of your spinal column.* Push, down, down. *Now hold that position. And let go.* Feel *your* back *and your* chest *going limp.*

Breathe *in and out. Now* relax *and let go.*

Each breath that you take helps your body to relax. Whenever you inhale, every muscle, each individual cell, is nourished and energized. Whenever you exhale, every muscle, each individual cell, is cleansed of impurities and tensions. Your body *and* your baby *are really enjoying this exercise.*

Now become aware of your shoulders *and your* neck *and all the tension that you store there. Begin to wash out this tension by pushing the tips of your shoulders up toward your ears;* push *until you feel as if you can almost touch your ears with your shoulders.*

Push, push, push. Hold *it. And let go.*

Breathe *in and out. Now relax and let go.*

Now lift your hands a few inches above your body and make a fist. *Tighten your fist.* Tighten, tighten, tighten. *Now* hold. *And let go.*

Breathe *in and out. Now relax and let go. Continue to breathe* deeply *and* evenly. *With each breath that you take, you choose to become more relaxed. You* feel comfortable *and* safe *and* secure.

Now become aware of your face. *Notice the muscles around your eyes, your mouth, and your jaw. Begin to squint your eyes. Tighten the muscles around your mouth. And tighten your jaw.* Tighten, tighten, tighten. Hold. *And let go.*

Breathe *in and out. Now relax and let go.*

Now that your body is relaxed, let your mind relax too. Don't work at it, just drift.

[LEAVE TWO MINUTES OF SILENCE ON THE TAPE, THEN CONTINUE.]

Now imagine yourself walking along a river-bank. Watch the water flowing by, swirling around rocks and lapping over the shore. The sound of the flowing water is rhythmic and relaxing. The wind blowing over the river feels cool and comfortable on your skin.

There is a lush, grassy meadow right next to the stream. It contains a wide variety of flowers, including violets, daisies, and wild red roses. At the edge of the meadow is a tangle of eucalyptus and all kinds of trees—towering oaks, gentle weeping willows, bristling pines, line after line of strong, gray birch, and more. This is a beautiful place, and you decide to lie down on the grass and take in all the splendor.

From all the flowers and trees that grow around you, choose one that you would most like to be. Then imagine yourself as a tiny seed inside that flower or tree.

Feel the warmth and moisture around you. Feel how safe and dark and cozy it is here. As you get used to being here, notice that you are growing. Allow yourself to really experience *this growth. Feel yourself expanding cell by cell. Just relax and watch yourself getting bigger and stronger. You have lots of time. Take all the time you need. Let the music carry you forward.*

[RECORD TEN MINUTES OF BAROQUE MUSIC AT THIS POINT ON THE TAPE. WHEN THE MUSIC IS COMPLETE, THE PERSON READING FOR THIS TAPE SHOULD RECORD THESE WORDS.]

Slowly return to a state of complete waking consciousness. First wiggle your fingers and toes. Now open your eyes. Remember to retain the feelings and images that have come to you during this exercise. Holding on to your experience, use all your senses from vision to hearing to touch to focus on your immediate surroundings. Now, sit up.

[THE TAPE ENDS HERE].

As the final part of this exercise, take a large sheet of white paper—for instance, the sort you get from an artist's sketch pad—and a box of crayons. Using images, symbols, or whatever comes to mind, translate onto paper the experience you have just had.

Even if you are convinced that "nothing happened," your drawings may reveal some of the emotions or sensations of your earliest life. For instance, you may glimpse the *colors* of the delivery room or understand the feelings of those present at your birth. So try to reserve your judgment until you have completed "The Seed" in full.

Exercise 14: Back to the Womb

THEME: Reexperiencing prenatal and birth feelings
INSTRUMENT: A book showing the unborn child at different phases of development, visualization technique
PARTICIPANTS: Mother
TEMPO: Thirty minutes, at least once this month

To conduct this exercise you will need a book showing color photographs of embryonic development through the nine months of pregnancy. We recommend the pictures found in Lennart Nilsson's *A Child Is Born*, Robert Rugh and Landrum B. Shettles's *From Conception to Birth*, or any similar book.

Begin by finding a comfortable chair or sofa in a quiet—and private—corner of your home. Spend about twenty to thirty minutes looking through the pictures in your chosen book. Imagine that you are looking at images of your own prenatal development, and immerse yourself in the sensations and feelings that you experience as a result.

After you have studied the pictures, lie back and play at least thirty minutes of the musical tape you created in Exercise 1. As you listen, focus on your memory of the pictures and on any spontaneous thoughts, feelings, or images that occur. Please do not force yourself to "remember" your experience in the womb or intentionally conjure up images of birth. Instead, just relax, listen to the music as you recall the pictures in the book, and let the mental images flow. Close your eyes and imagine the music carrying you back to the warm, moist enclosure of the womb.

This exercise may trigger prenatal or birth memories or feelings and images of womb life. You might, for instance, glimpse a color, hear the muffled sound of a voice, or perceive the image of a tiny baby swimming in amniotic waters. Or you may simply have the *feeling* of what it was like to be in the womb.

If you find that the exercise is a positive experience, we suggest that you repeat it again in about a week and after that, as often as you like. Images generated by the exercise often build on each other so that, after a while, a more complete picture of your prenatal experience begins to emerge. When you have done this exercise a couple of times, you might find it useful to follow it up with some right-brain doodling. What do your doodles tell you about the experience you may have had upon your entry into the world? What do they say about your feelings about the experience of *giving birth,* which you are about to go through?

Exercise 15: The Amniotic Sea

THEME: The sounds and sights of birth
INSTRUMENT: A radio, a warm bath, journal, a pencil, and visualization
PARTICIPANTS: Mother
TEMPO: Thirty minutes, at least once this month

For most people, the security experienced before birth may represent the deepest sense of safety and love they'll ever know. And now, with the help of an exercise suggested by Hayward, California, obstetrician Rene Van de Carr, you may be able to recapture the sensations of that forgotten, enriching time.

Begin on any quiet evening when you have at least thirty minutes to spend alone in the bath. Fill your bathtub with warm water. Turn your radio on at low volume, and set the tuner between stations so that you hear a constant, whooshing static. Remember not to touch the radio while you are in the water, unless it happens to be battery operated. Turn the lights off, and shut the blinds so that the room is dark.

As you sit in the dark, your senses bathed in warmth and in what psychologists term "white" noise, you will reexperience some *of the sensations of the womb. As you do, try to recreate in your mind the moment you left just such an environment to enter a colder, brighter, vaster terrain peopled by beings of immense proportion. Whether or not this exercise evokes a bona-fide birth memory, it will recreate for you, at least in a small way, the feeling of being born.*

After you have completed your bath, you might find it useful to follow it up with some right-brain writing. What do your words tell you about the experience you may have had upon your entry into the world? What do they say about your feelings concerning the experience of giving birth, *which you are about to go through?*

To elicit further feelings, write the following questions in your journal one at a time, then try to answer them without thinking. Answers may come to you in the form of a feeling, a sensation, a color, or words.

- *Was my mother awake when I was born?*
- *Did my mother say anything when I was born?*
- *Did a doctor or other attendant say anything when I was born?*
- *Did I feel welcome at my birth?*

- *Did I sense joy from those around me?*
- *Did I sense fear or trepidation from those around me?*
- *Did I sense relief from those around me?*
- *Did harsh lights bother me?*
- *Did my mother hold me?*
- *Was my father present?*
- *Did my father hold me?*

Remember, you may supplement this list in any way you wish. After each question, take a few moments to consider the psychological significance of the answer that comes to you. For instance, how might the perception that your parents felt fearful or joyful at your birth have influenced your emotional development throughout your life? Also, consider the overall tone of the answers you generate. Was your start in life nurturing or deflating? Do the images and feelings you have evoked reveal a happy family environment or one that was cold and confused?

After you have finished the three birth exercises above, you may, if you wish, try to validate your answers or impressions by checking with your mother, father, obstetrician, or hospital records.

Exercise 16: The Inner Circle

THEME: Harmonizing the mind
INSTRUMENTS: Paper and crayons or pastels
PARTICIPANTS: Mother and father
TEMPO: Fifteen minutes twice a week this month, then as often as you like

Throughout history, the circular drawings known as mandalas (samples shown below) have symbolized the human need for wholeness, order, and balance. In Tibetan Buddhism, the mandala is a ritual instrument, much like a mantra, used to assist meditation and concentration. Western practitioners have likened the concentric circles sometimes appearing in mandalas to the passage between different states of consciousness. The great psychiatrist Carl Jung even had his patients draw mandalas in order to help them put their conflicts in perspective. By imposing this ancient form on their individual fears and anxieties, Jung believed, his clients would see their own troubles from a broader, more *universal* point of view.

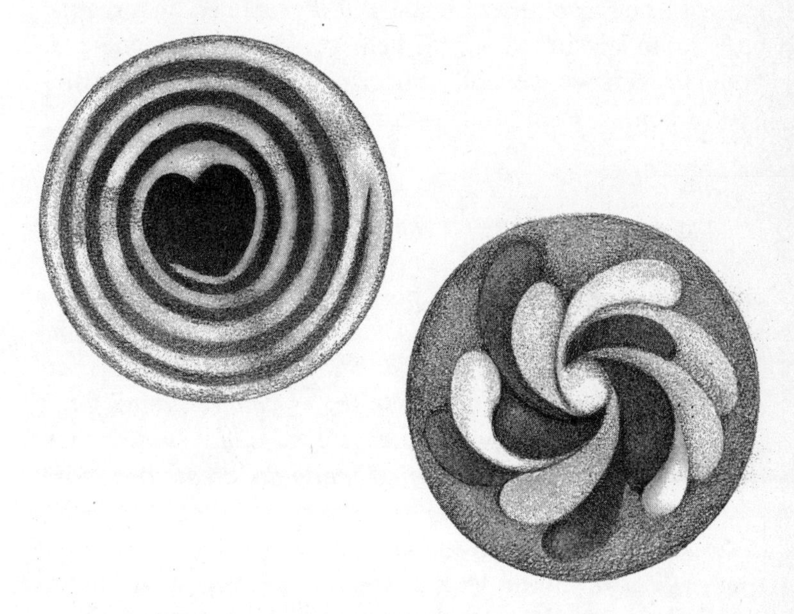

We have found that drawing mandalas *can* in fact promote a sense of well-being and aid in the process of self-discovery. The reason is this: As you create a mandala you will find yourself focusing on the circumscribed area of the drawing. This area, or field, will come to resemble a movie screen upon which your unconscious mind projects the details of your life. As you gaze at this screen, you may find you have arranged these life details in new and unusual ways. You may even find that you have expressed a trait or characteristic of which you were previously unaware. Whatever pattern or picture you ultimately create, however, will reveal a sense of internal order and balance. As you express this inner balance, you should achieve a sense of relaxation and calm.

This is particularly important at the end of Month Three, after the emotionally taxing effort to recall (on some level, at least) the sensations of birth. But if practiced on a regular basis, mandala drawing will help you focus your energies, maintain perspective, and achieve a sense of balance until—and of course, even after—your baby is born.

Take a large sheet of white paper. We suggest a sheet 12 by 18 inches but a similar size works just as well. Lay a plate or the lid of a pot on top of the paper. Draw the outline of the plate with a crayon, colored pencil, or paintbrush. Now take out your drawing tools and look at them. Pick a color and use it to draw something inside the circle. You can create anything you want—squiggles, triangles, squares, lines, faces, trees—anything. Be as spontaneous as possible. Immediately after you have finished your first mandala, create two more.

You may look at your mandala drawings, or you may put them aside. If you do look at them, you may try to understand their literal or symbolic meaning. Do they tell you anything about important people or events in your life? Do they say anything about your relationship to the child within you? You may prefer to forget about analysis and simply appreciate your mandala's artistic merit, or you may gaze at the patterns while thinking nothing at all.

Remember, it is not necessary—or even desirable—for you to try and figure out what your mandalas mean. Rather, it is the act of drawing—the *process*—that really counts. If you allow yourself free creative reign while drawing, you will enhance your sense of balance and internal harmony. By focusing on the task, you will discover hidden stores of order, energy, and strength.

Month Three Summary

New Techniques

12. Right-Brain Doodles	Accessing the right brain	10–30 minutes, whenever you feel the need to explore your feelings
13. The Seed	Guided imagery	60 minutes, once this month
14. Back to the Womb	Womb photos	30 minutes, once this month
15. The Amniotic Sea	Recreating the womb in the bathtub	30 minutes, once this month
16. The Inner Circle	Harmonizing the mind	15 minutes, twice weekly

Familiar Techniques to Continue

1. Viva Vivaldi	Music to grow by	60 minutes, twice weekly
2. Time Out for Mom	Relaxation	20 minutes, once a day

3. Daily Diary	Writing	Every day, as needed
4. Affirmations	Positive thinking	At least 2 minutes, twice daily
5. Dream Work	Understanding dreams	Every time you have a dream
6. Feast on a Star	Energy booster	Once a day, when needed
7. Hello, Baby	Communicating with the unborn baby	10–20 minutes, twice weekly
8. The Right-Brain Spin	Writing	40 minutes, when needed

Remember that the exercises listed above are merely suggestions. Practice as many or as few of the Womb Harmonics techniques as you wish. These exercises are meant to help you relax; they should not add to your stress.

Your Baby at Three Months' Gestation

WEEK	SIZE AND WEIGHT	EMBRYOLOGICAL, FUNCTIONAL, AND PSYCHOLOGICAL CHANGES
9	1.5 in. (3.7 cm) .14 oz (4 gm)	Teeth, fingernails, toenails, and hair follicles begin to develop. Skin thickens. Skeleton and muscles are growing rapidly now. The nerves supplying the eyes, the nose, the tongue, and the vestibular system for balance are all in place. External genitalia begin to differentiate males from females. When the eyelids and palms are touched, they react by closing. The unborn child responds to changes in the position of the mother.

10	2.1 in. (5.3 cm) .25 oz (7 gm)	The palate and the lungs are complete. The muscles of the digestive tract become functional. The gall bladder secretes bile, the external genitalia are well defined, and the brain has the basic organization it will have as an adult. If the forehead is touched, the unborn child turns his head away.
12	3 in. (7.5 cm) .5 oz (14 gm), the weight of an ordinary letter	The taste buds are structurally mature. The olfactory nerve, which governs the sense of smell, is fully developed. The lungs begin to expand and contract regularly. The thumb and the forefinger can be opposed to each other. All the major systems are formed. The unborn child can kick, turn his feet, curl his toes, frown, and purse his lips. If his lips are stroked, he responds by sucking. At the 12-week mark, unborn children begin to show individual variations, particularly in facial expressions. The sex of the baby is now apparent from external genitalia.

You at Three Months of Pregnancy

WEEK	THE PREGNANCY EXPERIENCE
9–10	Your waist slowly expands, and symptoms of early pregnancy, including frequent urination, breast tenderness, nausea, and tiredness, may persist. You probably have gained an average of between 1 and 2 pounds; symptoms of nausea, however, may have disrupted your appetite, causing you to lose weight.
11	Symptoms of early pregnancy, including frequent urina-

tion, breast tenderness, nausea, and tiredness, should begin to subside.

12 Symptoms of early pregnancy, including frequent urination, breast tenderness, nausea, and tiredness, disappear in most instances.

PART TWO

The Second Trimester

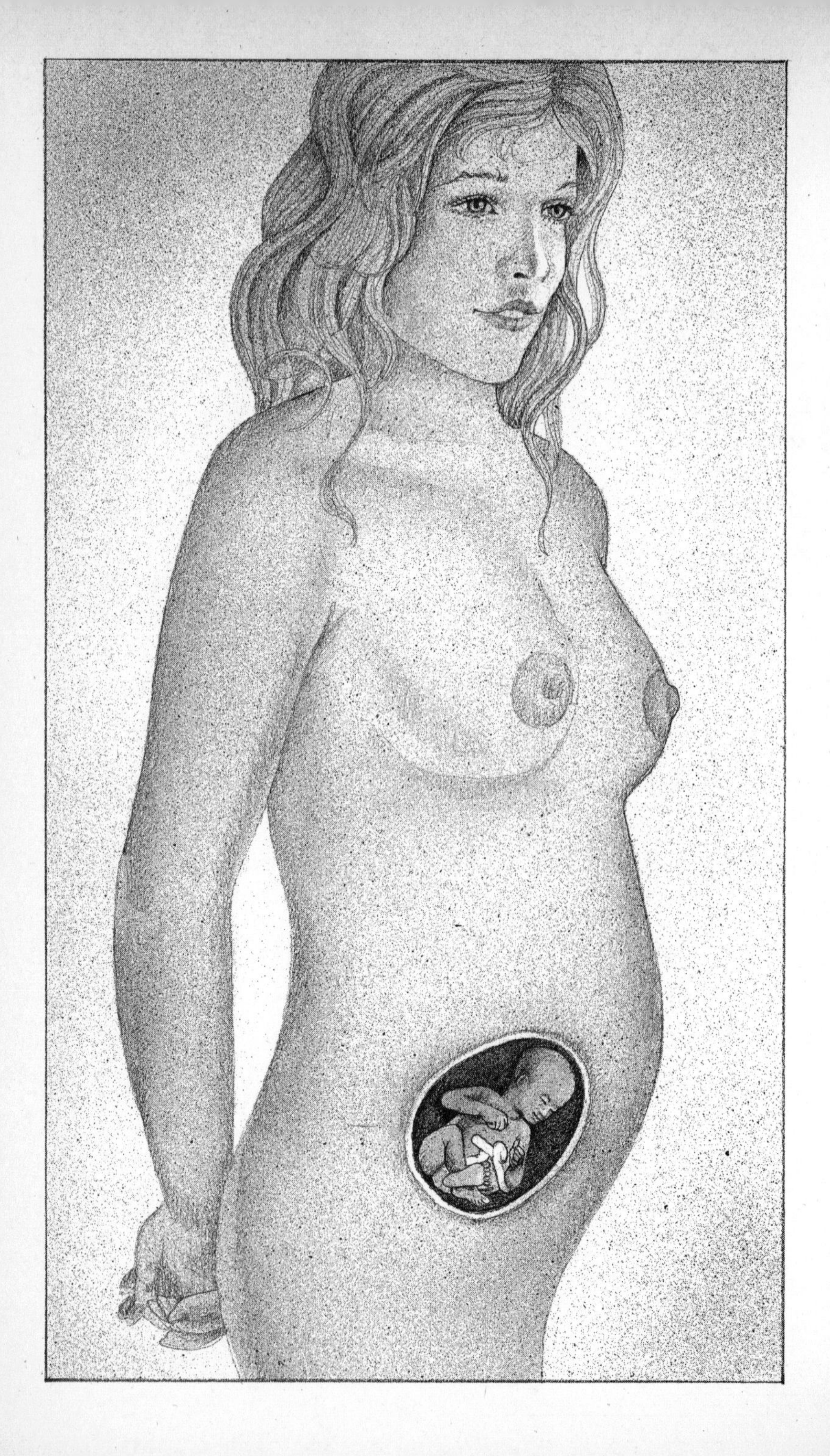

4

MONTH FOUR: Inner Bonding

You have now reached an important landmark in your pregnancy: the beginning of the second trimester. For most women, extreme exhaustion and morning sickness subside as new waves of energy and optimism kick in. Perhaps most important, during the second trimester your baby will be increasingly receptive to the world beyond the womb.

By now, your baby is so responsive that a bitter substance like quinine introduced into the amniotic fluid will cause her to cease drinking and frown. Introduce a sweet flavor, like saccharine and she will double her normal rate of ingestion. Your developing baby is so sensitive, she will react to tactile stimulation and loud sounds. Shine a light on your abdomen, and she will attempt to shield her eyes.

The four-month-old fetus also responds to sound in specific ways. Even the most agitated baby relaxes to Vivaldi. And even the calmest unborn child starts to boogie—that is, move and kick—if exposed to music with a lively, "up" beat. In fact, your baby's response to light, flavor, and music indicates that at four months' gestation, she may be capable of conditioned learning and seemingly intentional behavior. Analysis of brain structure shows that the four-month-old unborn has the neural circuitry—if not the capacity—for rudimentary memory as well.

The fourth month of pregnancy is an ideal time for *you* to become increasingly involved in the Womb Harmonics System too. The reason: The second trimester marks the point at which the risk of spontaneous abortion—otherwise known as miscarriage—drops to about two percent. This statistic is a relief for everyone; for the Womb Harmonics parent, it also signals the next phase in the process of bonding with the unborn. For now that chances of losing your baby are statistically low, you can go ahead and invest increasing amounts of emotional energy in soothing, stimulating, and communicating with your baby.

Most women who are or have been pregnant know the importance of prenatal bonding on an intuitive level. But recent research proves this intuitive knowledge correct. In a study conducted by clinical psychologist Kristen Van de Carr, for instance, parents who regularly practiced prenatal bonding techniques were compared with a control group of parents who did not. In general, Van de Carr says, "we found that the mothers who started to connect with their kids in the uterus had a deeper knowledge of their babies. As a result, the babies were easier to manage and the mothers were in a better frame of mind."

Anecdote after anecdote illustrates the truth behind these findings. One mother, for instance, recalls singing a Peter, Paul, and Mary song repeatedly during her pregnancy. After the birth of the boy, that lyrical song had a magical effect on him; no matter how hard he cried, whenever his mother started singing that song—and that song alone—he quieted down.

Increasing your emotional bond with your unborn child is a primary goal of Month Four. Toward that end, in "Heart to Heart" (Exercise 17), you picture your unborn child in detail, seeing every aspect of her being from her tiny fingers to her beating heart; you will ultimately create a psychological stream of energy between you and your baby. We also present Exercise 18—"Claying"—in which you and your spouse deepen your psychological connection to your child with clay. Finally, in "Getting to Know You" (Exercise 19), you will envision the nurturing relationship between you and your baby and ultimately embark upon a dialogue with your unborn child.

During the fourth month of pregnancy, you will also focus on your relationship with your partner. Having a baby should be a shared joy and responsibility. The exercises presented during this month will help you and your mate work toward that goal.

As your body continues to change shape, you may have at least fleeting doubts about your sexual attractiveness. You may worry about whether your partner still finds you sexy and whether he will remain faithful to you.

Your partner, on the other hand, may begin to worry about how he will fit into the new family equation. He may fear that you will become totally engrossed in the new baby, ignoring him. He may ask himself whether there will be enough love to go around.

Both you and your partner, moreover, may be concerned about finances, living space, and curtailment of freedom. Such anxieties can rock even the best of relationships, rendering a couple argumentative and tense.

To help you ease your tensions and understand the dynamics of your situation, we ask you and your partner, during Month Four, to examine your relationship in a completely open and honest way in "Moving Closer" (Exercise 21). For in our experience, only relationships that allow the expression of both positive and negative feelings can truly bloom. What's more, any improvements in your relationship with your partner right now will strengthen the family unit, providing a better, more positive model for your baby to emulate as she grows.

We also urge Month Four mothers to examine any fears they may have about the health and development of their babies. As the reality of pregnancy sets in, mothers may worry that things they did before conception or during the first trimester may affect their baby. Issues of concern may include such ordinary activities as the use of prescription drugs or alcohol, exposure to dental X rays, or even working with a computer or word processor. Moderate exposure to such things early in pregnancy rarely, if ever, affects the development of a baby, but can make the expectant mother anxious about her baby's health. Addressing this issue, "Whole and Healthy" (Exercise 20), will help you alleviate your anxieties and hopefully put them to rest.

Now that you have entered the second trimester of your pregnancy, it is especially important that you continue to carry out the core techniques mastered during the first three months. As in your first trimester, a primary goal for Month Four and beyond is to stay as relaxed as you can. This can best be achieved by listening to your music tape and by practicing alert progressive relaxation. To heighten your confidence and inner awareness, continue writing in your journal and recording your dreams. Whenever worries or anxieties set in, use the affirmation technique freely.

One last note: To help you embark upon your second trimester, we have included six important exercises. Please try each exercise at least twice and then continue using only those you find most helpful. If you do not have time to complete all the exercises during Month Four, do not worry. Simply fit them into your schedule when you can.

COPING WITH ANXIETY

We want to make it absolutely clear that all pregnant mothers worry. At the beginning of pregnancy they worry about the possibility of a miscarriage, later on about the likelihood of malformations and genetic defects. Before delivery, they worry about the complications of birth, the need for a cesarean section, and their ability to bond with the baby after she enters the world. Mothers and fathers fret over finances and living space for the baby. Women agonize about their weight gain. We could go on and on. The point is that these are normal anxieties. There is nothing wrong with you for thinking these thoughts. There is also nothing wrong with you if you have had fleeting thoughts of terminating your pregnancy, or if you have considered how inconvenient it is for you to be pregnant right now.

What we want you to avoid, however, are ongoing and severe doubts about having this baby, or strong and persistent feelings of rejection toward or dread of the child. These are potentially harmful feelings and should be dealt with in psychotherapy.

This book is meant to help you and your partner come to terms with the normal anxieties of pregnancy. The first step in lessening these normal anxieties is to simply acknowledge to yourself and your mate that in fact you harbor these feelings. Once you begin to face your fears honestly, they will have less power over you and you will feel increasingly confident and calm.

Exercise 17: Heart to Heart

THEME: Bonding with your unborn child
INSTRUMENT: Visualization
PARTICIPANTS: Mother and unborn child
TEMPO: Two minutes, every other day for the rest of the month, then as often as you like

You may do the following exercise after you have entered the state of alert progressive relaxation, or simply during a calm and quiet part of your day.

Before you begin, make sure that you are sitting in a comfortable position and that you have a few undisturbed minutes to yourself. Look down at your belly and visualize the baby within.

Picture your unborn child's tiny body, from the ten tiny fingers and ten tiny toes to the large head to the legs, curled and snug. Imagine the delicate features of your child's tiny face. See the mouth opening and closing and the eyelids moving in the warmth of the amniotic fluid all around. Now envision your baby's heart in the middle of her chest. See the heart beating, then picture the beating heart as a soft blue, pulsing liquid pool. Observe the depth and movement of that pulsing, living pool. Sense your baby's determination to thrive and grow, and realize that this new life force pulsing within you is completely unique. Now stop, hold your breath, and listen as your own heart beats in rhythm with the heart of your baby. Now start to breathe and listen to yourself breathing in and out, in and out. Envision your baby moving in rhythm with your breath. Sense the waves of love flowing between you and your baby. Watch your abdomen, and envi-

sion the baby within. Envision your baby's heart and your own connected by an everflowing, luminescent, pulsing, living stream.

Finally, turn your awareness to the room around you. You will experience a wonderful sense of warmth, peace, and well-being.

During Month Four, practice this exercise for a couple of minutes every other day. You may continue to use this technique throughout the nine-month program, however, whenever you want to establish a special emotional connection with the child in your womb.

Exercise 18: Claying

THEME: Deepening your psychological connection to your unborn child
INSTRUMENTS: Developmental photos or drawings, clay, and visualization technique
PARTICIPANTS: Mother, or mother and father
TEMPO: Thirty minutes, at least once a month, for the rest of the pregnancy

Before you do this exercise, go to any hobby or toy store and buy an ordinary piece of clay.

To begin, sit in a comfortable chair and look at pictures of the developing baby month by month up to the fourth month, where you are now. (You may use the drawings included in this book or any other book.) When you have finished studying the pictures, set them aside. Lie back and close your eyes.

Keeping your eyes closed, take the piece of clay in your hands and begin to play with it. As you do so, imagine that the clay is a fertilized egg undergoing rapid embryonic development until it reaches its present age. Imagine, in other words, that the clay represents the child in your womb at this moment. (At first you may feel a bit self-conscious relating to a piece of clay as if it were your unborn child. But if you can overcome your initial discomfort, you should find claying a delightful way to enhance your relationship with your baby.) When your "sculpture" has reached what you feel to be the four-month mark, open your eyes, look at it, hold it and cradle it, and tell it a story or sing it a song. Open yourself up to this tactile experience. Try to be as aware of your feelings as you possibly can.

Please feel free to repeat the claying exercise as often as you like throughout the duration of your pregnancy. By the way, you may also use a modified version of the claying technique, presented below, with your spouse. Remember to reassure your partner that, although the exercise might at first feel a bit silly, it is an excellent tool for deepening psychological connection to your unborn child.

Sit together in a comfortable spot, play some soft music, and study photos or drawings of embryonic development from conception through birth. But instead of imagining the clay as your unborn child, think of it as yourselves. Imagine being a sperm or ovum and moving through each state of embryonic development to birth. Imagine yourself as a single cell floating down your mother's fallopian tube toward the womb. Do you see the journey as joyous or frightening?

Envision yourself floating in the womb. Are the sounds that reach you comforting and melodious or jarring and harsh? Is the womb totally dark at all times, or do you sometimes see light? If so, what is the nature of this light? Is it brief and piercing or soft and luminous?

Imagine yourself coming into the world. Are the hands that receive you cold and intrusive or soft and gentle? As you and your partner immerse yourselves in this experience, you will come to identify with this imagined world—the world your unborn child inhabits right now. When you have both completed this claying activity, you can show each other what you have made and exchange thoughts and feelings.

We suggest that you and your partner do some form of the "Claying" exercise once a month. Each time you practice the exercise, spend the most time focusing on the part of the pregnancy you find yourself in at the moment. In this way, the exercise can help you have optimum empathy and identification with your unborn.

Exercise 19: Getting to Know You

THEME: Bonding with your unborn child
INSTRUMENTS: Visualization and affirmations
PARTICIPANTS: Mother and unborn child
TEMPO: Ten minutes, once a month, for the rest of the pregnancy

Do this exercise after you have entered the state of alert progressive relaxation, or simply during a calm and quiet part of your day.

Start by focusing all your attention on the child growing within you. Imagine that you have X-ray vision and that you can see through the abdominal wall and the placenta. As you penetrate your abdomen and placenta with your eyes, see your delicate, sensate baby floating freely, peacefully, in the expansive amniotic sea. Observe the large head, the tiny, curling fingers, and the little toes. See the luminescent, blue-white umbilical cord swirling from the placenta to the uterine wall. Now see globules of oxygen, vitamins, and nutrients gently flowing from your own bloodstream through the umbilical cord to your unborn. Focus on this image for a few seconds, then tell yourself: I am providing my baby with all the physical sustenance she needs. My own concern for our health and nutrition will enable her to grow up happy, healthy, and strong.

Now imagine that the tiny beads flowing through the umbilical cord carry not only food and oxygen but also profound love and warmth. See the minute spheres of positive energy and emotion flowing from your body through the umbilical cord to the baby in your womb. As this powerful maternal emotion flows into your baby, envision her responding with feelings of warmth, security, and love. As you send your love to the child within, she will feel your concern—and perceive your assurance that you want only what is best.

Now sense the emotion your baby is sending back toward you. Imagine that her feelings of warmth and security are encapsulated in minuscule bubbles traveling from her body through the umbilical cord into your very veins. Immerse yourself in the energy of this image, and feel the full force of the connection between you and the child growing within. Now pause and tell yourself: I am providing my baby with all the emotional sustenance she needs. My continuing concern for her well-being will enable her to have a happy, secure, productive life.

Now let this period of profound contact with your baby slowly come to an end. Softly, lovingly, release the intense psychological energy you are directing at the unborn. Close your eyes, and drift peacefully for a minute or two. As you drift, feel your body suffused with a warm, soft light. Now open your eyes, look around you, and wiggle your fingers and toes. And smile.

After you have completed this exercise, you will have a heightened sense of connection to your baby. The more you practice this exercise, the stronger your attachment to your unborn child is likely to become.

Exercise 20: Whole and Healthy

THEME: Overcoming fears about the health and well-being of your unborn child
INSTRUMENTS: Journal, affirmations, and visualization
PARTICIPANT: Mother
TEMPO: Thirty–forty-five minutes, once or twice this month

Naomi, a friend from Massachusetts, was rather upset. While vacationing on Cape Cod one weekend, she drank two margaritas. The next day, afflicted with a headache, she took four aspirins. A few weeks later, she discovered she was pregnant. Though Naomi had done nothing out of the ordinary—indeed, nothing that should have made her fearful for the safety of her baby—she began to worry that she had somehow disrupted the delicate development of the child within. Reviewing her actions during the first few weeks of her pregnancy, her anxiety increased: Before she'd known of the pregnancy, she remembered, she'd taken some allergy pills, used a microwave oven, and had had her carpets cleaned, filling her apartment with fumes. Instead of celebrating her pregnancy, Naomi was consumed by self-recrimination and apprehension.

The truth is, before a woman realizes she's pregnant, she may do any number of things that she would scrupulously avoid once her pregnancy has been confirmed. But if her behavior has consistently been moderate, she generally has nothing to fear.

Of course, most pregnant women worry—at some point, at least—about whether their baby will be healthy or deformed in any way. Many others harbor an unwarranted or excessive fear of miscarriage. Some are better able to cope with their worries than others. But even if fears do not haunt you as they did Naomi, they may emerge from time to time. Watching the news, for instance, you might hear of a child born blind or deaf or afflicted with multiple sclerosis, Tay-Sachs, or some other condition or disease. You may be successful in repressing your fears most of the time, but they will still be there.

The best way to conquer such worry is to face it head on. Once you have examined your inner anxieties, you will be able to put them in perspective and negative feelings will subside. Indeed, close examination will almost always reveal, as it did to Naomi, that your fears are unfounded. If your fears *are* grounded in reality—for instance, if you are worried about your diet, or about the medical philosophy expressed by your caretaker—confronting them will enable you to make changes for the good. You might, for example, improve your diet or find a doctor or midwife whose philosophy you share.

Last but not least, as you come to understand your fears you will realize that they also serve a positive function. For it is worry about the welfare of your baby that causes you to eat nutritious foods, abstain from alcohol, tobacco, and drugs, and get plenty of rest. It is this special concern for your child that has motivated you to follow the exercises in this book. As you face your fears, you will recognize that you have already assumed the responsible, committed attitude that will enable you to ensure the health and happiness of your baby when she is born.

To help you overcome excessive or undue worries about the health of your unborn, and to achieve a sense of realism and balance as you proceed with your pregnancy and your life, do the exercise below.

Sit in a comfortable spot with your journal during some quiet time of the day; make sure to instruct those around you that for a period of thirty to forty-five minutes, you must not be disturbed. Then close your eyes and ask yourself: What am I most afraid of concerning the health and safety of my unborn child? What, if any, are my deepest fears? *Let the answers pass through your mind for about five minutes, then open your eyes and describe your fears in your journal, writing anything that comes to mind. Then go back and read your fears aloud. After you have read this journal entry out loud once, do so again.*

Each time you pronounce a specific fear, imagine the word or phrase turning into a puff of smoke and dispersing in the air. Look up and, in your mind's eye, tell yourself: The likelihood that my baby will be less than whole and healthy is as remote and insubstantial as a puff of smoke. *Watch, in your mind's eye, as the smoke disintegrates. Then repeat your next fear aloud and watch it, too, disintegrate until you have banished all your fears in just that way.*

After you have dealt with the last of your fears this way, use the affirmation technique to help you feel confident and secure. First, say the following phrase aloud: My baby is whole and healthy in every way. *Repeat this phrase aloud ten times. Then turn to a blank page in your journal and write the phrase ten times.*

After you have finished, pull your clothing away so that the bare skin of your abdomen is exposed. Softly caress your pregnant abdomen and, in your mind's eye, gaze right through it so that you see your beautiful, healthy baby floating in the amniotic sea. In your mind's eye, count the fingers, one through ten. Then count ten toes. See the eyelids fluttering, the healthy feet kicking, and the tiny, healthy arms moving to and fro. As the image sharpens, once more caress your abdomen and say, You are whole and healthy in every way.

Now slowly and peacefully get up and continue with your day.

If you like, repeat this exercise once more in the course of the month. But we don't advise that you dwell on your fears. After you have dealt with them in the straightforward manner outlined above, it is best that you release them and, thus unburdened, go on to bathe your unborn child in warmth and love.

Some maternal anxiety is too great to be alleviated with the exercise above. If this is true for you, we suggest that you obtain an ultrasound scan of your baby, even if you would not otherwise do so. Of course, ultrasound scans should be used only when medically indicated; but we believe that high anxiety over your baby's health *is* a medical indication, and we would like to add it to the list of circumstances under which an ultrasound examination of the unborn can help. As you see the image of your baby on the monitor before your eyes, you will have evidence that she is as wonderfully healthy as can be.

Most ultrasound facilities will even allow you to take the image of your unborn child home. (If possible, make sure the facility you use has this capacity before making an appointment.) If you are able to obtain a take-home ultrasound image of your baby, you may perform the additional exercise below.

Put the ultrasound image of your baby up in a prominent position in your office or home. Look at the image as often as possible. Every time you look at the image, tell yourself: I now feel reassured that my baby is whole and healthy. *Then, look right through your abdomen with your mind's eye. But instead of merely envisioning an imaginary fetus, mentally impose the ultrasound image on your abdomen. As you "look through" your pregnant belly, see the baby from the ultrasound image wiggling her healthy fingers, waving her healthy arms, and turning her healthy head. Again tell yourself,* I now see that my baby is whole and healthy. *Repeat until you feel better.*

Exercise 21: Moving Closer

THEME: Deepening your emotional connection to your partner
INSTRUMENT: Partner dialogue, pen, and paper
PARTICIPANTS: Mother and father
TEMPO: Thirty minutes, at least once a week, for the rest of the pregnancy

Ideally, pregnancy is a period of shared joy for both you and your partner. Most couples who are about to have a baby, however, are also under stress. As your pregnancy proceeds, you may wonder whether your partner still finds you attractive. Your partner, on the other hand, may worry about marshaling the commitment and constancy he will need to parent his child once she is born. Moreover, you and your partner may harbor previous resentments that remain unsolved.

Because the quality of your relationship with your partner forms the emotional climate into which your baby is born, it is crucial to deal with any problems *now.* The fourth month of pregnancy is a good time to explore the strengths and weaknesses of your relationship as honestly and openly as possible.

Some people don't believe in making waves. Subscribing to "the ostrich philosophy of life," they prefer to ignore their troubles and hide their heads in the sand. But our experience shows that only relationships in which both positive and negative feelings are expressed can flourish and grow. What's more, many studies show that a good relationship between pregnant women and their partners leads to easier pregnancies and a healthier baby at the time of birth.

To help you ease your tensions and grow increasingly closer to your partner, do this partner dialogue. In this exercise, you will ask each other a series of specific, probing questions. Through these directed conversations, you will deepen your emotional connection as you sort out your feelings and fears.

Find a convenient, quiet time for you and your partner to sit down and spend at least thirty minutes together. This will be your opportunity to discuss your feelings about each other and the upcoming birth. Since it is best to repeat this exercise weekly, try to agree on a definite time that is convenient for both of you on a regular basis. The important thing is to keep this date even if one or both of you feels you have nothing to say. Believe us, something will come up.

Here are the ground rules for the dialogue:

- *Tell the truth.*
- *Speak from the heart.*
- *Share your feelings.*
- *Really* listen *to what your partner is saying.*
- *Be supportive.*
- *Do not interrupt.*
- *Do not make your partner feel guilty for what he is saying, and try to avoid feelings of guilt within yourself.*
- *Forgive yourself and your partner.*
- *Look into your partner's eyes while sharing thoughts and feelings.*
- *Take responsibility for your own feelings.*

Now you are ready to begin. In your first partner dialogue, both of you should complete the following phrases in your respective journals. (Your partner may use a sheet of paper if he does not keep a journal.) Write the answers down privately, before you discuss them with each other. Try to be as explicit as you can, but single words or phrases are all right too.

- *What I appreciate about you is:*
- *What I resent about you is:*
- *In the past, I have hurt you by:*
- *In the past, you have hurt me by:*
- *Am I ready to forgive you?*

Please stop for a few minutes and discuss your answers. Then return to your paper to complete this phrase:

- *I am still afraid to tell you:*

Now put down your papers and discuss your answer to the last question. Remember the ground rules of discussion.

Special Note: In the weeks and months that follow, you will spend your weekly dialogue time discussing a variety of issues. For instance, you might look at the way your parents related to each other when you were children. Do you see any similarities between your respective families? Is the way you relate to each other affected by the way your parents related years ago? You might even tackle such issues as the responsibilities and fears of parenthood or your feelings about the upcoming birth. Create and answer your own questions in your diary whenever you wish.

Exercise 22: Voluptuous and Sexy

THEME: Deepening your emotional and physical connection to your partner
INSTRUMENTS: Full-length mirror, affirmations, and partner dialogue
PARTICIPANTS: Mother and father
TEMPO: Repeat affirmations whenever necessary, and spend sixty minutes on the *complete* exercise once this month

As your body changes shape, you, like most other pregnant women, may have at least fleeting doubts about your attractiveness. In fact, it's easy for the pregnant woman to feel as if she has metamorphosed into a totally different species, especially as the pregnancy goes on. The shape you assume during pregnancy is drastically at odds with the slender, athletic ideal established by Madison Avenue, complete with running shorts and sneakers, business suit and briefcase, or strapless sequined gown. Given the dichotomy, you *may* feel a bit out of step. You may also ask yourself whether your partner still finds you sexually desirable, or whether he looks at other women in a different way than he did before.

To counteract such feelings, it is important that you come to see your pregnant body as beautiful and sexy. It is also important that you get your feelings out into the open by honestly discussing your sexual relationship with your partner.

Conduct the first part of this exercise alone, in front of a full-length mirror. Take off your clothes and look carefully at your pregnant body. Notice the sensual, rounded curve of your belly and the full, darkened regions of your breasts. Stand in front of the mirror for at least five minutes, examining your body from head to toe. Observe how your body has changed over the months. Close your eyes and remember your body the way it was just four months ago. Now open your eyes and look at your body the way it is now. Do you think that you still look attractive? Do you view yourself as too small? Too big? Do you think you've gained just the right amount of weight, or a bit too much? Do you find your pregnant body, with its expanding curves, sensuous and voluptuous? What do you like most about your pregnant body? What do you like least about it? Close your eyes once more and imagine your body the way it was four months ago. Now, in your mind's eye, see your body changing from its non-pregnant state to the pregnant state it is in now. Open your eyes, and once more study your body from head to toe. If your observations do not help you to feel good about your body, repeat the affirmations that appeal to you as often as you like:

- *My body is beautiful.*
- *My skin is glowing and radiant.*
- *Pregnancy is a deeply sensual experience.*
- *I feel more feminine than ever.*
- *My sexual desires are strong and alive.*
- *I am a strong, healthy, beautiful woman.*

For the second part of this exercise, conduct the following dialogue during your customary weekly discussion period with your partner. Before you start the conversation part of this session, you and your partner should answer the following questions in your respective journals. (Your partner may use a sheet of paper if he does not keep a journal.)

- *My worst sexual experience was:*
- *My best sexual experience was:*
- *What I like most about our sex life is:*
- *What I dislike most about our sex life is:*
- *Do I always communicate my sexual desires and needs?*
- *Are there any sexual thoughts or fantasies I have not shared with my partner?*
- *Do I sometimes use sex to express my anger, frustration, insecurity, or fear?*

After answering these questions, put your paper down and discuss your answers with your partner.

Month Four Summary

New Techniques

17. Heart to Heart	Using visualization to bond with the unborn	2 minutes every other day this month, then as needed
18. Claying	Using clay to bond with the unborn	30 minutes once a month
19. Getting to Know You	Communicating with the unborn through visualization and affirmation	10 minutes once a month
20. Whole and Healthy	Alleviating anxiety about your baby's health and well-being	30–45 minutes once a month
21. Moving Closer	Understanding your spouse	30 minutes, weekly
22. Voluptuous and Sexy	Improving your body image and achieving sexual intimacy with your partner	Once this month, then as needed

Familiar Techniques to Continue

1. Viva Vivaldi	Music to grow by	60 minutes, twice weekly
2. Time Out for Mom	Relaxation	20 minutes, once a day
3. Daily Diary	Writing	Every day, as needed
4. Affirmations	Positive thinking	At least 2 minutes, twice daily
5. Dream Work	Understanding dreams	Every time you have a dream
7. Hello, Baby	Communicating with the unborn baby	10–20 minutes, twice weekly

16. The Inner Circle	Harmonizing the mind	15 minutes, twice weekly

Your Baby at Four Months' Gestation

WEEK	SIZE AND WEIGHT	EMBRYOLOGICAL, FUNCTIONAL, AND PSYCHOLOGICAL CHANGES
16	6 in. (15 cm) 4 oz (112 gm)	During this period of maximum growth, your baby's heart has become fully developed with a pulse rate of 120 to 160 beats a minute. The eyes are now sensitive to light, and the surface of the brain has formed many convolutions. The spinal nerves and nerve roots acquire myelin, a sign of advancing development. Your unborn child's skeleton is now detectable via X ray. And the growth of fine body hair, called *lanugo,* has begun. Your baby will now react to a bitter substance such as iodine in the amniotic fluid by ceasing to swallow and by frowning. She will react to a sweet substance (saccharine) by doubling her normal rate of ingestion. Your unborn child senses and reacts to cold fluids and tickling. Shine a light on your abdomen, and your baby shields her eyes. Make a loud noise, and she covers her ears. She can also grasp her umbilical cord and suck her thumb. Many experts believe that by the sixteenth week of gestation, your baby is capable of conditioned learning, rudimentary memory, and even intentional behavior.

You at Four Months of Pregnancy

WEEK	THE PREGNANCY EXPERIENCE
14	Your breasts may darken as pigmentation increases. A dark line may appear between your navel and pubic bone. Abdominal enlargement becomes apparent, and you can actually *feel* your womb between the pubic bone and navel.
14–15	If you have already had a baby, you become aware of fetal movements about now.
16	If this is your first pregnancy, you should become aware of fetal movements this week or next.

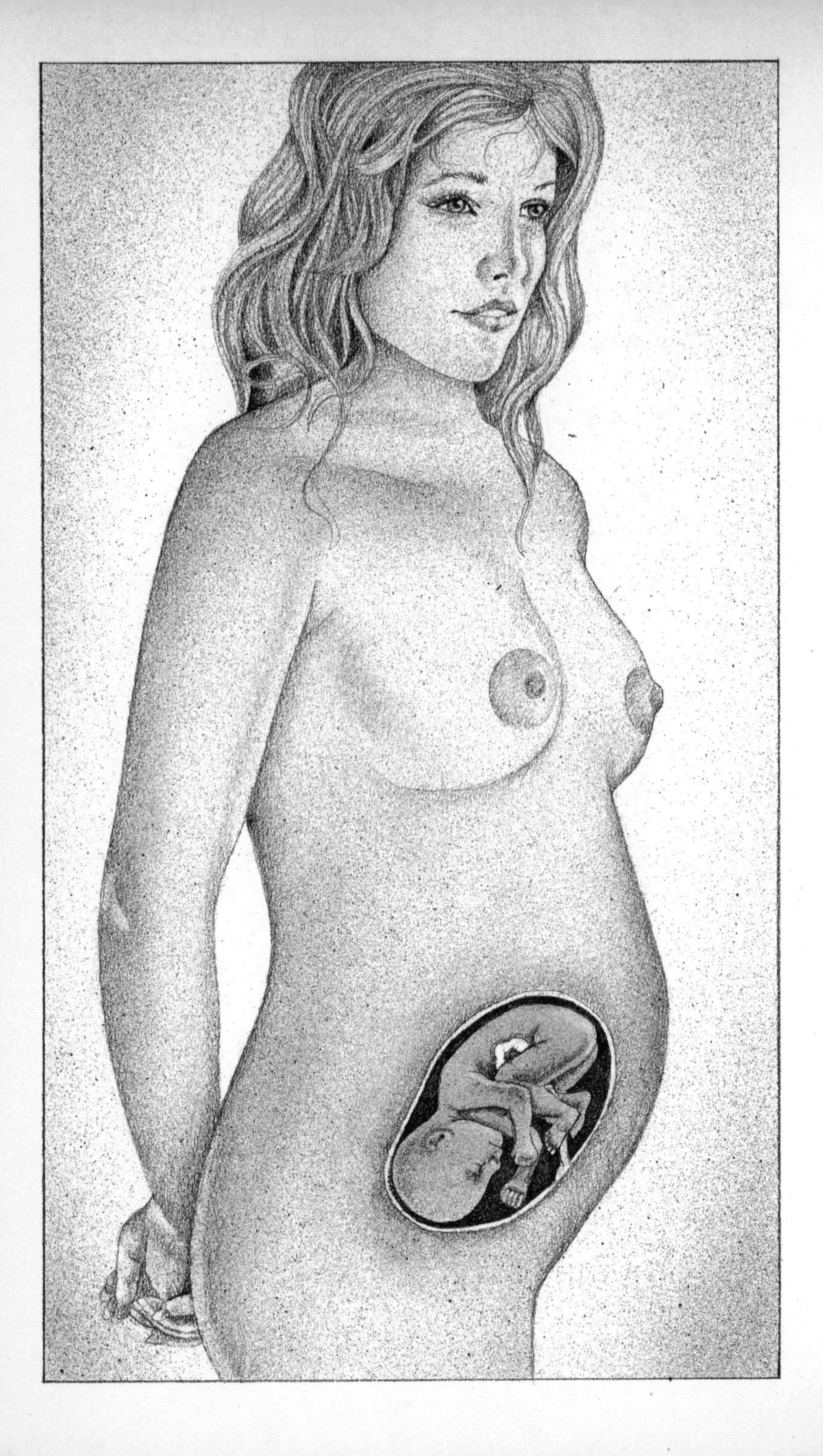

5

Month Five: The Umbilical Telephone

You are now midway through your pregnancy. You can feel your baby kick and turn—and you may even hear him hiccup through the abdominal wall. Your baby, for his part, is starting to wake up to the world. He has a strong kick. He alternates periods of activity with periods of drowsiness and sleep. And, if born right now, he might live and even eventually thrive. Indeed, Marcus Richardson of Cincinnati was eighteen weeks old (halfway through the fifth month of gestation) when he became the youngest baby ever to survive premature birth in 1971.

For the Womb Harmonics parent, however, the most fascinating aspect of development may be the unborn child's sense of hearing. With the hearing apparatus virtually formed, your unborn child has now begun to establish a perceptual hook-up to the outside world. The importance of this auditory link has been documented in dozens of anecdotes and a spate of impressive research studies.

Canadian conductor Boris Brott, for instance, says his interest in music began in the womb. "This may sound strange, but music has been a part of me since before birth," Brott explains. "As a young man, I was mystified by this ability I had to play certain pieces sight unseen. I'd be conducting a score for the first time and, suddenly, the cello line would jump out at me: I'd know the flow of the piece even before I turned the page of the score. One day, I mentioned this to my mother, who is a professional cellist. I thought she'd be intrigued because it was always the cello line that was so distinct in my mind. She was; but when she heard what the pieces were, the mystery quickly solved itself. All the scores I knew sight unseen were ones she had played when she was pregnant with me."

Brott is not alone. One woman was surprised one day to find her two-year-old daughter sitting on the living-room floor, chanting to herself, "Breathe in, breathe out, breathe in, breathe out." The woman said she recognized the words immediately—they were part of a Lamaze exercise she'd practiced during the last weeks of her pregnancy. She had not uttered those words since.

These anecdotal reports are backed up by research in both the field and the laboratory. In a recent study, for instance, psychologist Peter Hepper of Queens University at Belfast in Northern Ireland determined that some children may even become soap opera fans in the womb! Hepper studied fourteen pregnant women; half of them religiously watched *Neighbors,* a daily Australian soap opera popular in the United Kingdom. The other half of the women did not watch the show at all. When the children were born, six out of seven in the first group became quiet and alert when they heard the theme tune. Only two in the second group had a similar reaction.

In another series of studies, psychologist Anthony DeCasper at the University of North Carolina at Greensboro showed that human newborns actually recognize speech they heard while in the womb. DeCasper asked sixteen pregnant women to tape-record their reading of three different children's stories: *The King, the Mice, and the Cheese* and two different versions of *The Cat in the Hat.* During the last six and a half weeks of pregnancy, a third of the women read the first story aloud three times a day; a third read the second story aloud three times a day; and a third read the last story aloud three times a day. When the babies were born, DeCasper and colleagues offered each infant a choice between the story his or her mother had repeatedly read and one of the other two stories.

To enable babies to cast their votes, DeCasper invented the "suck-o-meter"—a nipple hooked up to a computerized sound system in such a way that a baby can switch between two taped voices simply by changing the rhythm of his sucking. The findings? Shortly after birth, when the babies were tested, thirteen of the sixteen adjusted their sucking rhythm to hear the familiar story as opposed to the unfamiliar one. DeCasper had shown that newborns recall speech sounds that they heard before birth.

In yet another study, DeCasper demonstrated that a newborn not only recognizes specific speech sounds, but can actually identify his *own mother's voice.* DeCasper did this study with the help of ten new mothers at the Moses Cone Hospital in Greensboro. Each mother taped herself reading *To Think That I Saw It on Mulberry Street* by Dr. Seuss. DeCasper then had each newborn choose—via the suck-o-meter—between his own mother's tape and a tape made by one of the other mothers. Nine of the ten infants indicated a preference for the tape made by their own mothers. To rule out the possibility that the babies were simply responding to the mother's voice heard *after* birth, DeCasper performed the same experiment with fathers. Babies *do* show a preference for the father's voice several weeks after birth—but, the study proved, at two days of age, babies indicate no such preference. The implication is that preference for the mother's voice develops long before birth, in the womb.

Your baby's sense of hearing will not evolve fully until

the last trimester of pregnancy, but the fifth month is a good time to start talking and singing to the unborn. As your baby's sense of hearing becomes increasingly acute, your voice will be a constant and gentle encouragement for his growth.

Three important exercises can help you communicate with your baby through sound: "Sweet Melodies" (Exercise 24), in which you sing to the unborn child; "Story Time" (Exercise 25), in which you read to the unborn child; and "Small Talk" (Exercise 26), in which you tell your baby about everything from an interesting magazine story to your deepest feelings.

During Month Five, we also introduce a second, far more rapid means of inducing deep relaxation. Relaxation is just as important as ever, but you now have many techniques to practice on a monthly basis. Considering that you have a life—including a career and/or family—to contend with as well, some days might feel especially full. In those instances, we suggest that you spend five minutes on Exercise 23, "Quick into the Deep," instead of thirty minutes on the alert progressive relaxation technique presented in "Time Out for Mom" in Month One.

Finally, to round out the program for your fifth month of pregnancy, we present "Creative Daydreaming" (Exercise 27), in which you construct your own guided-imagery script to offset any negative dreams or fears. The script you create will help you to immerse yourself in an intense, dreamlike state while still awake. Replacing negative images with positive ones while in this slightly altered state will help you to resolve your worries and cope more effectively with life.

In addition to this specialized dream exercise, it is important that you continue to recall your dreams and record them in your journal, as instructed during Month One. As you record your dreams in the second trimester, you may find that some of your dream images have changed. The research conducted by dream psychologist Patricia Maybruck reveals that while small animals often represent the unborn child early in pregnancy, the same baby during the second and third trimester may be represented by large plants—even jungles—and by large animals, including wolves, tigers, or dinosaurs. While a small house or cottage may have represented your womb early in your pregnancy, dream images representing your expanding waistline might include large buildings, skyscrapers, or huge underground caves. Note the way your dreams have changed. Also, remember that the meaning of all dream imagery is ultimately personal, varying widely from one individual to the next. Do not accept interpretations of your dreams unless they feel right to you.

Please persist in practicing all your core exercises, summarized for your convenience on page 116. It is most important that you continue to write in your journal, listen to your special music, and maintain the weekly dialogues (from "Moving Closer") with your partner.

We know that you will enjoy singing and talking to your unborn. The songs, stories, and conversations you introduce this month will help to nurture your baby throughout the pregnancy—and perhaps even throughout life.

Exercise 23: Quick into the Deep

THEME: Quickly entering the state of deep relaxation
INSTRUMENT: Self-hypnosis
PARTICIPANT: Mother
TEMPO: Five minutes

As your pregnancy—and your progress through the Womb Harmonics System—advances, you will spend more time with your unborn baby. As you establish a special emotional bond with your child, your focus will increasingly turn to the life within. Like most pregnant women today, moreover, you are probably a busy person, with a career or other small children or both.

For these reasons, we present this five-minute exercise. You may use this quick-relaxation technique on a daily basis as a substitute for the complete alert progressive relaxation exercise. You may also use the quick relaxation technique to prepare yourself for exercises involving visualization or guided imagery.

Start by lying down or sitting in a large, comfortable chair. Make sure you have at least five minutes of private time, enough to complete this exercise.

After you have assumed a comfortable position, become aware of three things in your visual field. For instance, you might choose an antique brass clock, your favorite poster, and this book. Any *three objects will do.*

After you have noticed three elements in your visual field, shift your attention to three sensations in your body. For instance, you may focus on the feel of a velveteen chair against your skin, the tingling aftertaste of the toothpaste you just used, and the rhythmic movement of your chest as you breathe. Any *three sensations will do.*

After you have focused on three sensations in your body, shift your attention to three sounds in your environment. You may notice the tick-tick-tick *of the clock, the sound of a TV in the next room, and the patter of rain outside.* Any *three sounds will do.*

Now close your eyes. In your mind, see two of the three objects; feel two of the three bodily sensations; and tune in to two of the three sounds. Finally, keeping your eyes closed, focus on only one of the visual images; one of the bodily sensations; and one of the sounds.

You are now ready to relax. You may use this time to just drift, to complete a visualization or guided-imagery exercise, or to work on a dream or problem.

Exercise 24: Sweet Melodies

THEME: Communicating with your unborn child through song
INSTRUMENTS: One or two of your favorite songs
PARTICIPANTS: Mother, father, and unborn child
TEMPO: At least once a day for the rest of the pregnancy

Ever since the first month of your pregnancy, you have been playing a cassette tape containing some of your favorite music. The sounds and vibrations of the tape have helped you relax and, reaching the inner recesses of the womb, have soothed and stimulated your unborn child as well. Now that your baby has reached the fifth month of gestation, however, his hearing apparatus is firmly in place. What's more, he is learning to distinguish *your* voice—and perhaps your partner's voice—from all the other sounds and voices reaching the womb. This makes it the perfect time for you to start communicating with your baby through song.

You and your partner can sing or hum to your unborn child even if your voices are not particularly beautiful—even if you can't carry a tune. The important thing is not that your song is of professional quality, but that it establishes your presence and communicates your love and caring to the unborn.

Choose one or two soft, soothing songs that you would like to sing to your baby on a regular basis. You may choose an old Beatles love song (such as "All My Loving," "And I Love Her," or "Eight Days a Week"), or a folk song that you find particularly cheerful and warm. Songs by Judy Collins, Donovan, or Peter, Paul and Mary can work well. You may also select some favorite children's songs, such as "The Wheels on the Bus" or "Baby Beluga." If you have trouble finding a suitable song, look for inspiration in the albums of Raffi and the Rise and Shine Band; Sharon, Lois and Bram; or Larry Groce and the Disneyland Children's Sing-Along Chorus. Choose a song that is lively without being jarring, and soothing without being so relaxing it puts your baby to sleep.

Sing to your baby as often as you like, the more the better. Remember that babies love repetition, so sing the same song or two over and over for the rest of your pregnancy. Your child will learn to associate your songs with your loving support. Don't be surprised if the songs you have chosen continue to have a powerful, positive effect on your child long after birth.

Exercise 25: Story Time

THEME: Communicating with your unborn child through storytelling
INSTRUMENT: A favorite story or a couple of favorite nursery rhymes
PARTICIPANTS: Mother, father, and unborn child
TEMPO: Once a day for the rest of the pregnancy

Regularly reading to your baby in the womb gives him a feeling of security and warmth. If you read the same story over and over, you will sensitize your baby's nervous system to linguistic patterns, introducing a touchstone through which he may feel welcome and safe after birth.

Choose one children's story or two nursery rhymes or poems that you find particularly pleasant. Since you and your partner will be reading these selections almost every day for the rest of your pregnancy, choose wisely. Make sure the pieces you select are rich and colorful and fun. Above all, pick a story or poem that is gentle and loving. Stay away from violent subjects and overly dramatic readings. We have found that a number of stories by Dr. Seuss, including The Cat in the Hat, One Fish, Two Fish, *and* Green Eggs and Ham, *are particularly effective. We also recommend* Good Night Moon *by Margaret Wise Brown;* A Fly Went By *by Mike McClintock;* The Little Engine that Could *by Watty Piper; and* Madeline *by Ludwig Bemelmans. Recommended Mother Goose rhymes include "Little Bo Peep," "Little Boy Blue," and "Twinkle, Twinkle Little Star."*

You and your spouse may choose the same selection or different ones. After you have made your choices, you should each read your story or poem to your unborn child once a day.

After you have practiced the "Story Time" exercise for about a month, try to discern whether any specific words or phrases produce a predictable response on the part of your unborn child. Does a particular word or phrase cause him to kick almost every time? Does a certain section of the story produce a period of calm? Does your baby react differently to the different stories? To your voice and to the voice of your spouse?

Exercise 26: Small Talk

THEME: Communicating with your unborn child through conversation
INSTRUMENT: Talking
PARTICIPANTS: Mother, father, siblings (if any), and unborn child
TEMPO: Every day for the rest of the pregnancy

In order to get acquainted with your unborn child, it is important that you engage him in conversation each and every day. As you are driving to work, as you do chores around the house, just talk to your baby as if he were a small child of two or three. You may discuss any subject that is on your mind. If you have a fight with your partner, explain it to your baby; most important, make sure he understands that the argument in no way lessens the love you and your mate feel for him. *If you've had a hard day at the office, you might say,* I've had a bad day today. That's why I'm in such a bad mood. But this mood will pass, and it has nothing to do with you. I can't wait until you're born. I love you very much. *Describe to your unborn child the relatives and friends who are awaiting his arrival. As you chat with your baby, use language that is gentle, loving, and adult. There is no need to use baby talk. And avoid harsh, angry tones or shouting.*

If you are in a public place where you cannot easily or comfortably talk aloud, communicate with your unborn child through thought. This, too, will help you feel a sense of closeness to your baby. If your spouse and your other children want to talk aloud to the unborn child, encourage them to do so. If your partner is to be away for more than a few days, he may prepare some taped messages for the unborn child. Though he may at first find this approach somewhat embarrassing, assure him that you will play these tapes only when you are totally alone. Explain that the sound of his voice will help his unborn child maintain a bond with him even when he is gone.

Exercise 27: Creative Daydreaming

THEME: Easing anxiety and deepening your psychological connection to the unborn

INSTRUMENTS: Dream work, affirmations, and guided imagery

PARTICIPANTS: Mother

TEMPO: Thirty minutes before bed and for thirty minutes in the morning, at least once or twice a month for the rest of the pregnancy

By now, you have spent a few months recording and interpreting your dreams. Your dream work has in all likelihood helped you tune into your unconscious mind and gain increased perspective about what you feel and who you are. Now that you have become familiar with the language of your dreams, you can engage in additional exercises to help you ease your anxieties and communicate with the unborn. In the exercise below (adapted from psychologist Patricia Maybruck), you will use waking dreams to ease anxiety and bond with the unborn.

Before you go to bed, take out your journal and record any negative thought that may have passed through your mind earlier in the day. Then take the negative thought and turn it into a positive statement, or affirmation. For instance, if you were worried about the health of your unborn child, you might formulate the statement: My concern about my unborn child has helped me to maintain an excellent diet and to abstain from smoking, alcohol, unnecessary medications, and drugs. *If you worried about the expanding size of your body, you might say:* The changing shape of my body shows me that my baby is growing healthy and strong. *Write the affirmation down. Finally, as you learned to do during Month One, vow that you will remember your dreams as you are drifting off to sleep.*

The following steps may induce a dream about the issue that has been troubling you, leading to some sort of resolution. Whether or not that occurs, however, take the time to remember and record your dreams before getting out of bed in the morning.

During the day, find time to sit down for some journal work. Compose your own guided-imagery exercise based on your dream images and the affirmation you constructed the night before. Using last night's affirmation as your plot, create a dreamlike fantasy that puts a positive cast on your worries and doubts. For instance, let's say that last night you worried about the effect your changing shape will have on your relationship with your husband. Your affirmation might have gone something like this: As our child grows inside me, my husband will love me more and more.

Your guided imagery, based on this idea and the dream images, might go like this: It is a warm spring day and my husband and I decide to visit the park. We walk to the boathouse and rent a rowboat. He rows while I relax. Then I row while he relaxes. Eventually we reach the middle of the lake. We both stop rowing and simply drift. My husband looks down and caresses my stomach. "You're beautiful, and our baby will be beautiful just like you," he says to me lovingly. Then we hold each other, feeling suffused with joy.

After you write down your own guided-imagery script, read it aloud into a tape recorder. Later, when you do the alert progressive relaxation, listen to the tape recording of this guided-imagery script. Listen to this tape recording whenever you think it will ease anxiety or enhance your mood. Feel free to embellish or extend the script in your mind each time you listen to the tape.

Month Five Summary

New Techniques

23. Quick into the Deep	Deep relaxation	5 minutes, whenever needed
24. Sweet Melodies	Singing to the baby	Every day
25. Story Time	Telling stories to the baby	Every day
26. Small Talk	Talking to the baby	Every day

27. Creative Day-dreaming	Bonding with your baby through waking dreams	30 minutes before bed and upon waking, twice monthly

Familiar Techniques to Continue

1. Viva Vivaldi	Music to grow by	60 minutes, twice weekly
2. Time Out for Mom	Relaxation	20 minutes, once a day
3. Daily Diary	Writing	Every day, as needed
4. Affirmations	Positive thinking	At least 2 minutes, twice daily
5. Dream Work	Understanding dreams	Every time you have a dream
7. Hello, Baby	Communicating with the baby	10–20 minutes, twice weekly
16. The Inner Circle	Harmonizing the mind	15 minutes, twice weekly
21. Moving Closer	Understanding your partner	30 minutes, weekly

Your Baby at Five Months' Gestation

WEEK	SIZE AND WEIGHT	EMBRYOLOGICAL, FUNCTIONAL, AND PSYCHOLOGICAL CHANGES
18	7 in. (18 cm) 7 oz (190 gms)	The earliest possible point at which the developing child can survive outside the womb. Hiccups are audible and visible through the abdominal wall, and brain waves show increasing sophistication.

		Heart sounds are audible with a fetoscope.
20	7.75 in. (20 cm) 10 oz (240 gms)	The hearing apparatus is complete. The hands develop a strong grip. Crying patterns of premature babies can be identified through comparison with the mother's voice print. The neck region of the spinal cord has become myelinated. The baby kicks and turns and may occasionally cry audibly. Your unborn child is as sensitive to touch as a one-year-old. He will react to music or loud noise and discriminates between different sounds. Periods of drowsiness and sleep alternate with periods of activity.

You at Five Months of Pregnancy

WEEK	THE PREGNANCY EXPERIENCE
17	If you have not yet become aware of your baby's movements, you should do so now.
18	You may become increasingly aware of the painless, irregular tightenings of the uterus, otherwise known as Baxton-Hicks contractions. Your womb may now be felt at the navel level.

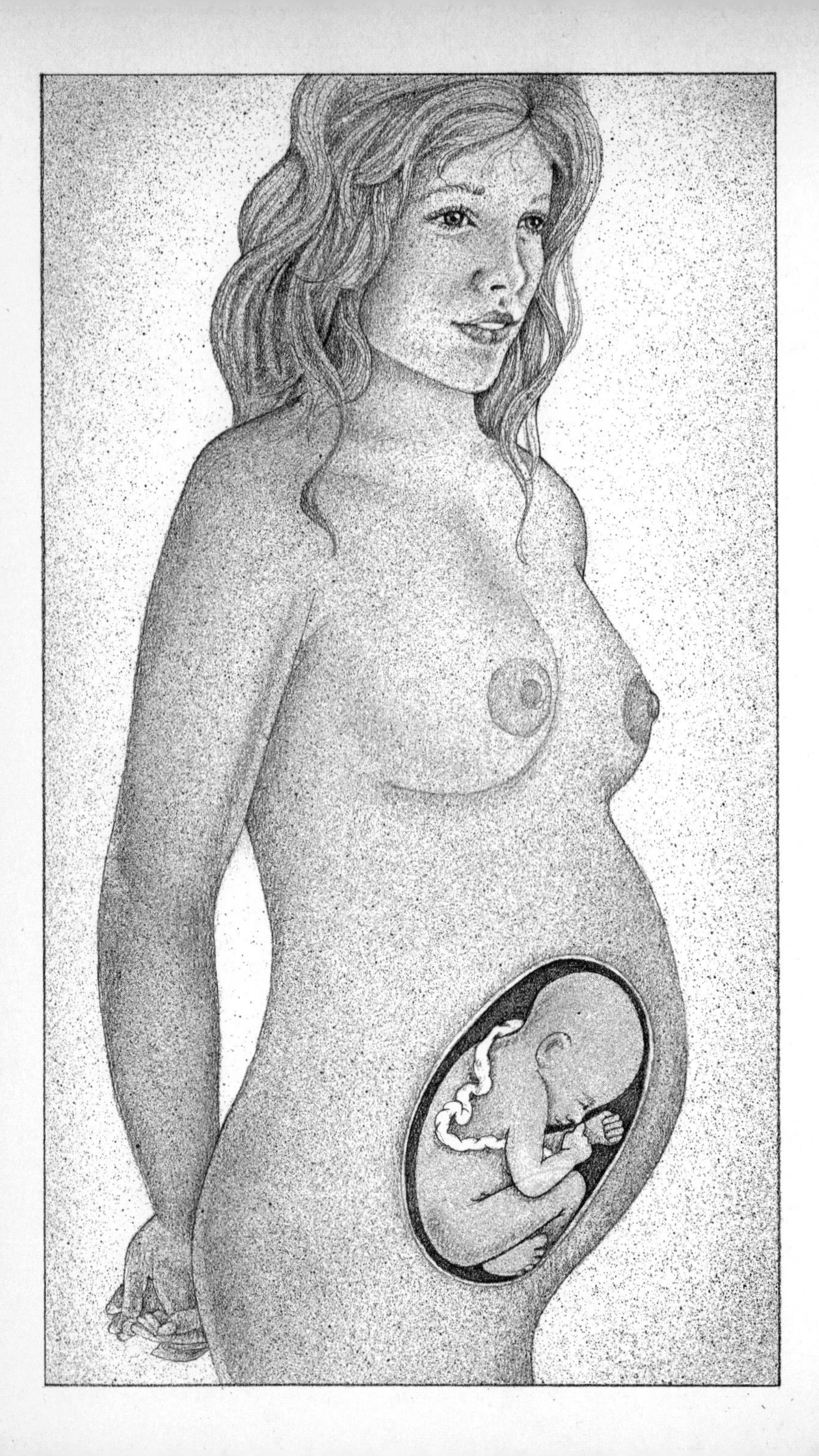

6

MONTH SIX: The Loving Touch

Feeling your unborn child move is always exhilarating. And by the sixth month of pregnancy, those kicks and somersaults, twists and turns, should feel much more powerful—much more emphatic—than they did before. You have known all along that your baby is mobile and sensate. At twelve weeks after conception, you may recall, she kicked, turned her feet, and curled her toes. But now that your baby is larger, you are more likely to feel even more movements along the abdominal wall.

Your baby, meanwhile, has been exercising her sense of touch and motion all along. By the seventh week after conception, she was responding to your twists and turns with movements of her own. At sixteen weeks, as her sense of touch developed, she began to suck her thumb. As her tactile perceptions sharpened, she increasingly used them to explore her aquatic universe, comfort herself, and develop coordination and strength.

In short, your baby's senses of touch and motion have been at work for a long time. Now that *you* can feel the everyday movements your baby initiates, however, you have an opportunity to communicate back and forth—to send a direct, tactile message to the womb and to receive a direct response.

Communicating with the unborn through touch is as old as humanity itself. Pregnant women have stroked and massaged their abdomens since ancient times. More recently, the wisdom of this ancient practice has been affirmed through the study of newborns. Anthropologists, for instance, report that societies in which infants are frequently massaged and held are more cooperative, less violent places to live.

These reports are backed up by human and animal studies. Some of the first solid proof that tactile stimulation is crucial for the newborn came from animal scientist Harry Harlow back in the 1950s. Harlow allowed infant monkeys to choose between two surrogate "mothers"—a soft, terry-cloth model without food and a hard, wire model with food. The monkeys always chose the terry-cloth "mother," even though it meant not eating. What's more, in subsequent experiments, monkeys allowed contact only with the wire surrogate showed a failure to thrive, while those exposed only to the terry-cloth surrogate were virtually normal.

Researchers know that human infants deprived of normal physical contact fail to thrive as well. What's more, studies indicate, extra tactile stimulation—in the form of a gentle, loving massage—can enhance a baby's ability to respond and relax. In a study conducted by Dr. Susan Ludington-Hoe, for instance, 120 babies were stroked for a hundred extra minutes over the first three days of life. These babies gained weight faster and performed motor movements earlier than a control group that did not receive the extra contact.

In light of this research, it's no wonder that pregnant women have a natural maternal urge to stroke the child within. Although no controlled studies have yet been done, all evidence indicates that gentle tactile stimulation benefits the unborn child as well.

To tune into the movements of your unborn child, first of all, follow the instructions in "Tiny Dancer" (Exercise 28). After you have learned to discern your baby's subtlest movements, we teach you to communicate with your unborn child through movement and dance in "Waltzing with Baby" (Exercise 29). Once you and your unborn child have developed mutual awareness through these exercises, you may go on to the "massage dialogues" (Exercises 30 and 31). In the first dialogue, you communicate with your child through massage and music; in the second dialogue, you use the technique of creative visualization as well.

In addition to our four tactile exercises, you will learn during Month Six a dream-incubation technique for communicating with your baby through dreams. Month Six concludes with "Your Sacred Place" (Exercise 33), a special exercise for seeking emotional balance and keeping in touch with your spiritual self. Whether or not you are religious is immaterial for this exercise. As virtually all gurus, shamans, and other assorted sages have pointed out through the ages, beyond the material universe of our senses lies an abiding metaphysical, transpersonal, spiritual realm. The last exercise of Month Six may help you find this realm within yourself.

In addition to the new Month Six repertoire, continue to practice the core Womb Harmonics techniques: deep relaxation, journal writing, dream work, partner dialogues, and talking and singing to the unborn.

Exercise 28: Tiny Dancer

THEME: Tuning in to your baby's movements
INSTRUMENT: Quiet concentration
PARTICIPANTS: Mother and unborn child
TEMPO: Twenty–thirty minutes, twice a day

The first step in establishing a tactile line of communication with your unborn child is tuning in to her movements. Do so twice a day, first in the morning before you get out of bed and again right before you fall asleep. To sense your baby's movements, recline on your left or right side. Keep one hand on your abdomen, and concentrate. As you feel your baby moving, just count the movements, one by one.

Some babies are naturally quieter than others in the womb. (Ultrasound studies show that, depending on the baby and the trimester, fetal movements range from 200 to 700 a day.) Some women are naturally more sensitive to these movements than others. Your baby's movements may seem to have the power of a linebacker's kick, or the gentle subtlety of a butterfly's flutter. You may feel ten tiny quivers a day or a hundred thunderous claps. No matter—these physiological differences have nothing to do with either your baby's health or yours. Do not feel concerned if your child does not seem to be an acrobat in the womb; as long as you feel *some* movement each day, all is fine.

Dr. Eliahu Sadovsky of Hadassah University Hospital in Jerusalem, one of the world's experts on fetal movement, adds that after the twenty-seventh week of pregnancy, you should be able to detect at least five movements during each thirty-minute period. If you detect fewer than three movements, keep counting for an hour or more. If you count fewer than ten movements in twelve hours or fewer than three movements in eight hours, contact your obstetrician. A severe slackening off of fetal movement may be an early warning that your baby is under stress. As the womb gets more crowded in the eighth and ninth months, the unborn child moves less and less.

Exercise 29: Waltzing with Baby

THEME: Communicating with your unborn child through dance
INSTRUMENTS: Musical tapes and your body
PARTICIPANTS: Mother, father, and unborn child
TEMPO: Ten to twenty minutes, at least once or twice a week for the rest of the pregnancy

Almost from the time your baby was conceived, she has sensed your movements through space. Every time you stood up, took a walk, or traveled by bus or train, your unborn child sensed your shifts in rhythm, position, and speed. In short, you have been communicating with your unborn child through movement for months.

One of the most pleasurable forms of movement, of course, is embodied in dance. Many dance therapists believe that movement and dance are the basis of awareness. The deep emotions flooding our unconscious mind, they say, will often remain hidden until they find expression through the muscles in our face and shoulders, arms, and legs. How often have you yourself been unaware of your feelings until your body and breathing muscles rearranged themselves in patterns of joy or anger, ecstasy or fear? Though muscle patterns change in response to extreme internal states almost instantly, you may guard your feelings from conscious awareness for months or years. Changes in muscle patterns —including the movements associated with dance—are often precursors to conscious feelings.

Because of the deep connection between movement and emotion, dance is an excellent way to communicate your feelings to the unborn. Before you begin the dance exercise below, put on some loose and comfortable clothing and select music appropriate to this exercise. The waltzes of Strauss or the ballet music of Tchaikovsky are particularly effective, especially Strauss's *Blue Danube* and *Emperor Waltz* and Tchaikovsky's *Nutcracker Suite.* If you prefer, you may use any of the numerous rhythmic, melodious pieces by Mozart, Vivaldi, or Schubert. You may also choose a suitable contemporary piece. Avoid at all cost hard, driving rock music and discordant jazz pieces!

One last note: As you conduct the exercises below, stay in tune with your baby's reaction to the music. If you love a piece but your unborn child reacts with anxiety—exhibited through increased and unpleasant kicking—omit this selection for a while and introduce it a few days or weeks later to see if your baby's reaction has changed.

Feel free to use one, two, or all three of the techniques presented below. As long as you take note of our guidelines, you may adapt these exercises to fit your own energy level, life-style, and taste.

Dance Technique One

Choose a rhythmic, joyful, flowing composition—a waltz is ideal—and move so that you explore the music as a sound and feeling in your body. Do not attempt to perform actual dance steps unless these come to you very naturally. Instead, let the uplifting, joyous mood of the music filter through to all the muscles in your body—from your toes and ankles through your legs, buttocks, and back to your arms, shoulders, and head—in a spontaneous, organic way. Continue to dance in this natural fashion until the mood of the music penetrates not just your muscles but your inner emotional self.

Dance Technique Two

Choose a moving, lilting musical composition or ballad and dance slowly with your mate. As you dance, touch each other. We also suggest that you and your partner both massage your pregnant abdomen, communicating your love and devotion to your unborn child.

Dance Technique Three

The slow, round, snakelike movements of belly dancing should be particularly soothing to both you and your unborn child. You don't have to be an expert belly dancer to benefit from this technique; all you have to do is approximate belly-dancing motions. Ideal for this exercise is the Arabian section of the Nutcracker Suite. *You can also buy special belly-dancing music in most large music stores. To begin, just play your musical selection and roll your head, shoulders, and hips, making wavelike movements with your arms. If you are comfortable doing so, elaborate your belly-dancing technique by raising your arms above your head. Continue to belly dance until you feel tension drain from your body, leaving you relaxed. If your spouse feels like it, he may participate in belly-dancing sessions as well.*

Exercise 30: First Massage Dialogue

THEME: Tactile communication with the unborn child
INSTRUMENTS: Movement, massage, and music or voice
PARTICIPANTS: Mother, father, siblings, and unborn child
TEMPO: Ten minutes, twice a week, for the rest of your pregnancy

Your unborn baby has been soothed by a sort of massage almost from conception. When she was smaller than a dime, when her senses of sight and hearing were still undeveloped, amniotic fluid washed over her in gentle waves. As she grew larger, she began to feel the firm grip of the uterine wall.

Now, in the sixth month of gestation, your baby is big enough for you to feel her flutters and kicks. At this point, she can feel *your* hand move along the abdominal wall too. If you lovingly caress your abdomen, your unborn child will sense that touch and respond to it by moving in a slow and luxurious fashion as relaxation and warmth set in.

Whenever you feel your baby kick, stroke your abdomen as gently and lovingly as possible. Sit or lie in a comfortable position that you can more or less maintain for about ten minutes. Then conduct the massage through a series of long, broad strokes from below your belly button to below your breasts, or through a series of broad circular motions covering roughly the same area. This simple technique will help you soothe your baby, slowing down her movements and communicating a message of love.

To heighten this special period of communication, you may want to rub your abdomen with a light natural oil. Although our massage exercise is completely effective without the oil, a lubricant will enhance the movement of your hand over your abdomen. We suggest that you use a cold-pressed fruit or vegetable oil made without any additives or chemicals—coconut oil and almond oil are ideal.

As you massage your unborn child, you may also want to play soothing music, speak softly, or sing. Any of the songs or compositions recommended throughout the book are appropriate. The gentle, consistent rhythm you create with your hands and your voice will enable your baby to sense your love and to feel confident and secure.

Research shows that women who receive massages during pregnancy have easier labors and are more responsive to their infants after they are born. So get your spouse or a professional massage therapist to give you a massage as often as possible. Indulge yourself. You deserve it!

Exercise 31: Second Massage Dialogue

THEME: Tactile communication with the unborn child
INSTRUMENTS: Movement, massage, and visualization
PARTICIPANTS: Mother, father, and unborn child
TEMPO: At least once this month, then whenever you want, in place of the first massage dialogue, throughout the rest of your pregnancy

Begin by assuming a comfortable position that you will be able to maintain for about ten minutes. Perform the massage through a series of long broad strokes from below your belly button to below your breasts, or through a series of broad circular motions covering roughly the same area. You may want to rub your skin with a light natural fruit or vegetable oil before you begin.

But instead of augmenting your massage with music, song, or speech, use the visualization technique. As you massage your unborn child, close your eyes and imagine that you can see through the abdominal wall with your hand. Moving your hand like a sensitive electronic scanner, envision the uterus and your unborn child within. Feel and see the shape of your baby's body in your mind's eye. Is your baby asleep or awake? Active or quiet? See how your baby responds to the motion of your hand and the sensation that you are actively there.

Now visualize a stream of light emanating from your hand and reaching through the uterus to the child within. Picture this stream of light as a powerful message of love. Does your baby respond in any particular way to this image of light? If so, how?

Visualize the stream of light as a pathway through which your feelings and those of your unborn child can easily pass. As you continue to massage your abdomen, imagine that you are actually softly touching your baby's back and chest, her arms and legs. If your child is upset, soothe her with your touch. If she is happy, enter that happiness with her, moving your hand in rhythm with the joy you sense she feels. As you move your hand in rhythm with your child, feel the intensity of the moment increase. Let the full power of your love travel down the stream of light into the uterus, and feel your baby's sense of love and security travel through the stream of light into your gently moving hand.

As the massage session slowly comes to an end, lift your hand to a position about twelve inches above your pregnant uterus. Slowly lift your hand higher and feel your connection to the child within. After a few seconds, become aware of your own breathing and wiggle your fingers and toes. Keeping your eyes closed, become increasingly aware of your own body and the room it inhabits.

Now open your eyes. Look down at your body and look around the room. Feel the sense of peace and love that permeates every corner of the room. Look down at your hand, and remember the special emotional connection it recently made with the unborn. Now get up and go about the rest of your day. But every time you look at your hand, you will be reminded of the love that flowed through it from you to your unborn child and from your unborn child to you.

Exercise 32: Dreaming of Baby

THEME: Establishing a closer connection to your unborn child through dreams
INSTRUMENTS: Dream work and journal
PARTICIPANTS: Mother and unborn child
TEMPO: Once or twice a week, for the rest of the pregnancy

This month, you learn to communicate with your unborn child through your dreams. The method is called *dream incubation,* a form of dream control that has been practiced all over the world in one way or another since ancient times. In ancient cultures, dreamers often induced desired dreams or invoked specific dream characters and images by spending days in a special environment where they could meditate and perform elaborate rituals. But dream incubation need not be so complex. If you follow our directions, you will easily and comfortably establish a tighter bond with your unborn child through conversations, images, and actions in your dreams.

Begin by reflecting on the emotional ambience of your sleep environment. Is it warm and nurturing, filled with pictures of your family, cherished personal objects, books and plants? Is your bedroom quiet, with adequate ventilation—cool in the summer and warm in the winter? As you study your bedroom, ask yourself whether it adequately expresses the positive aspects of your personality and marital relationship. What, if anything, does it say about your feelings toward the child growing within?

After you have considered these issues, make your dream room as calm and comfortable as possible. If you have a loving picture of yourself and your mate, consider displaying it in a prominent position. Surround yourself with objects that express positive aspects of your life and personality, as well as photographs or posters that give you an inner sense of joy and calm. Finally, find a few objects or images that you associate with your unborn child and place them near your bed. You may, for instance, choose a picture of a baby at six months' gestation; a tiny article of clothing; or the special books you read aloud to your baby every day.

You have now created a sleep ambience conducive to inducing positive, loving dreams about the unborn. Before you go to sleep, sit quietly in your bedroom and focus on the baby growing within. Caress your abdomen, and say to yourself, Tonight I will meet my unborn child in my dreams. *Look at and handle the objects that remind you of your unborn child, and focus on the meeting you intend to have in your dream; banish all other images and thoughts from your mind. Once more say,* Tonight I will meet my unborn child in my dreams. *Then take your journal and write the sentence down. If you wish, you may also draw a picture that expresses your intent. As soon as you're finished, turn off the light and allow yourself to drift off to sleep. As you fall asleep, continue to focus on your sentence and/or picture and on the special objects and images you have placed around the room. Remind yourself that tonight you will remember all dreams related to your baby.*

Upon waking, before you move or open your eyes, concentrate on recalling your most recent dream. If it does not involve your baby, follow the images in your mind backward in time until you recover a dream involving your unborn child. Record this dream and any other dream you may have had immediately after you open your eyes. Keep in mind that you may be dreaming about your baby in a symbolic form. Therefore, write down every detail of your dreams and then try to unravel them.

These instructions should enable you to encounter your unborn child in your dreams. According to psychologist Patricia Maybruck, one woman who used a similar induction technique dreamed that she and her unborn child inhabited the uterus together. "We were floating or swimming underwater, but I could breathe and talk," the woman relates in Maybruck's book, *Pregnancy and Dreams.* "It was amazing. The water was pale blue and our baby was glowing pink. The cord was sort of a turquoise color, luminescent. It was breathtaking, so beautiful. . . . I woke up with a feeling of reverence and gratitude for this wonderful miracle." Whatever your *own* dream is like, dream induction will help you express your deepest feelings to your baby. As your feelings are revealed through dream images, the mother-child bond will grow increasingly strong.

Exercise 33: Your Sacred Place

THEME: Connecting with your deepest self
INSTRUMENTS: Visualization and guided imagery
PARTICIPANTS: Mother and father
TEMPO: Ten minutes at least once this month, then whenever needed for the rest of the pregnancy

Somewhere within you is a sacred place—the internal equivalent of a chapel, sanctuary, or temple. To discover your own sacred place, close your eyes and envision a journey by plane, train, or magic carpet. Imagine yourself traveling through mountains and valleys, past cities and over oceans, until you feel you have arrived. Now see your sacred place in detail. Is it an endless, underground cavern carpeted with lush green grass and daisies? The inside of an Egyptian pyramid, with hieroglyphics and ancient artifacts? A room painted floor to ceiling with water lilies in the style of Monet? Or is it the attic of your family home, piled with heirlooms, old letters, and your grandmother's floppy hats? Whatever your sacred place, envision yourself there now.

Once you have completed this visualization, have someone read to you the guided-imagery induction, below. If you do not have anyone to read it to you, record the instructions on a tape recorder and play them back to yourself at the appropriate time.

> Once you have entered your sacred place, become aware of a beam of sunlight above you. Walk into the warm shimmering light and let it bathe you inside and outside. As you stand there, think of any negative thoughts or feelings that you have been struggling with. Allow the sunlight to wash away these worries and disturbing ideas.

If there are any paintings or statues of deities or guides in your sanctuary, talk to them now. Describe your problems or worries, and ask for guidance. If you feel like it, offer a gift of thanks. When you are ready, come out into the here and now.

Look around and remember the magical details of your sacred place. You can return to this peaceful, internal realm to put your mind at ease whenever you feel the need.

Month Six Summary

New Techniques

28. Tiny Dancer	Sensing your baby's motion	Every day
29. Waltzing with Baby	Communicating with your baby through dance	10–20 minutes, twice weekly
30. First Massage Dialogue	Communicating with your baby through massage and music	10 minutes, 2 to 5 times a week
31. Second Massage Dialogue	Communicating with your baby through massage and visualization	Once this month, then as needed
32. Dreaming of Baby	Bonding with your baby through dreams	Once or twice weekly
33. Your Sacred Place	Connecting with your inner emotions	10 minutes this month, then as needed

Familiar Techniques to Continue

1. Viva Vivaldi	Music to grow by	60 minutes, twice weekly
2. Time Out for Mom	Relaxation	20 minutes, once a day
3. Daily Diary	Writing	Every day, as needed
4. Affirmations	Positive thinking	At least 2 minutes, twice daily
5. Dream Work	Understanding dreams	Every time you have a dream
7. Hello, Baby	Communicating with the baby	10–20 minutes, twice weekly
16. The Inner Circle	Harmonizing the mind	15 minutes, twice weekly
21. Moving Closer	Understanding your partner	30 minutes, weekly
24. Sweet Melodies	Singing to the baby	Every day
25. Story Time	Telling stories to the baby	Every day
26. Small Talk	Talking to the baby	Every day

Your Baby at Six Months' Gestation

WEEK	SIZE AND WEIGHT	EMBRYOLOGICAL, FUNCTIONAL, AND PSYCHOLOGICAL CHANGES
24	10–12 in. (25–30 cm) 1.25 lbs	Your unborn child, now a miniature human being, more than doubles her weight this month. Her eyelids open and close, and fee-

(500 gm)	ble respiratory movements begin. From six months on, scientists record the rapid eye movement we associate with dreams. Your baby listens to sounds attentively, with attention apparently keyed to the maternal heartbeat. During the sixth month, researchers report, some developing babies show signs of discomfort or stress. Special signals include violent shifts in body position, frantic kicking, unusual weight loss or weight gain, and too much thumb sucking.

You at Six Months of Pregnancy

WEEK	THE PREGNANCY EXPERIENCE
21	Your baby's movements continue to accumulate vigor and force. With the increased size of your lower abdomen, you may find it a bit more difficult to move around.
22	Your period of greatest weight gain begins now.
23	Your heart and lungs are now doing about 50 percent more work. Body fluids increase, causing you to sweat more than usual. Blood circulation increases, causing you to flush easily and giving you that wonderful, pregnant glow.

PART THREE

The Third Trimester

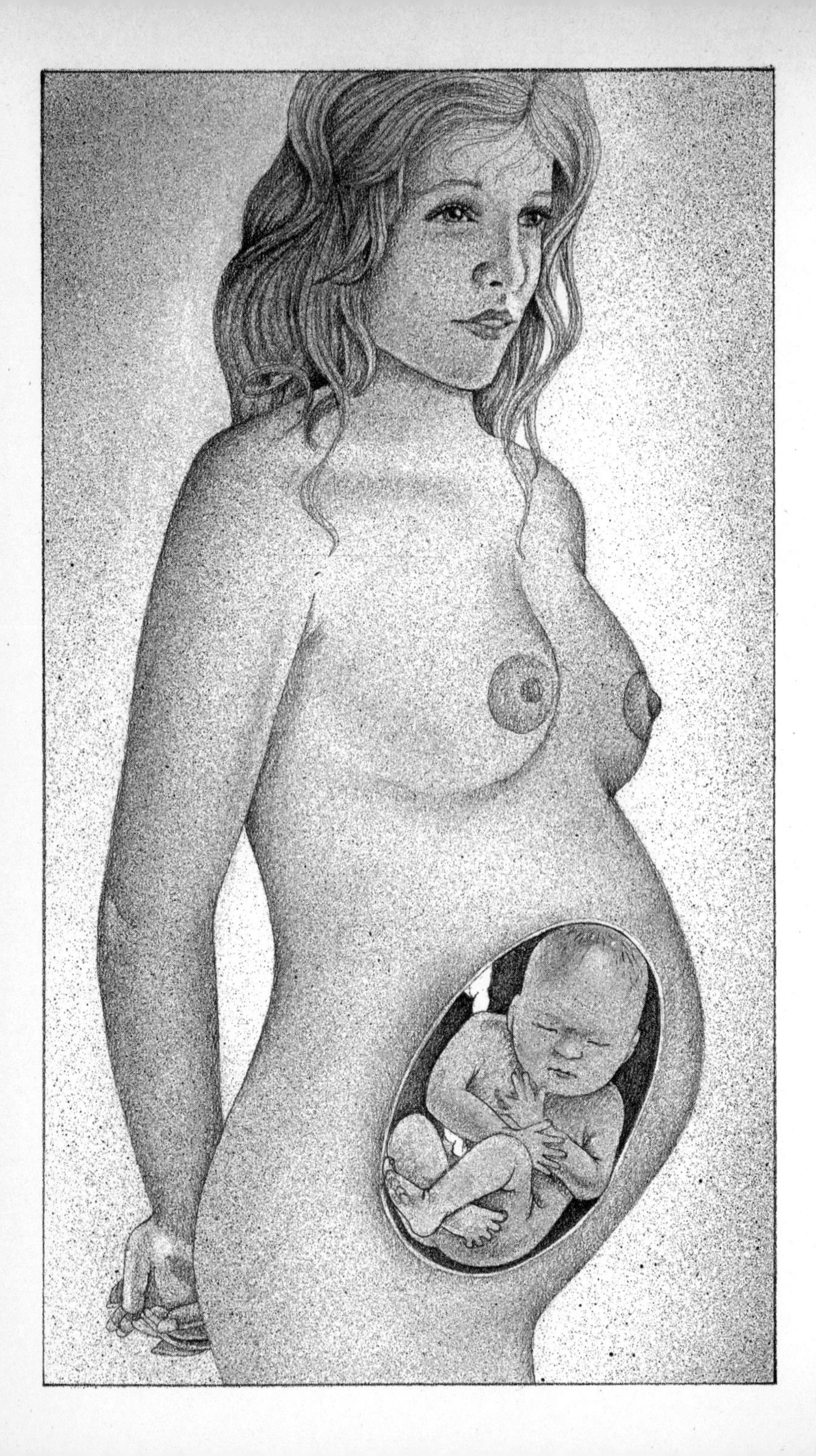

7

MONTH SEVEN: Consciousness Rising

Congratulations! You and your baby have just entered the third trimester. In a little more than twelve weeks, your baby will be born.

During Month Seven, your unborn child will really take on a personality of his own. Not only will he be able to move in rhythm to music, he will, if given the chance, show preference for one composer or style of music over another. He will become increasingly attuned to your voice, your movement, your touch.

According to recent scientific studies, in fact, the seven-month-old unborn baby is even capable of conditioned learning—that is, he will respond to a variety of stimuli in predictable ways. A particularly striking example of this ability was demonstrated by Dr. Michael Lieberman, who studied pregnant smokers. Lieberman showed that the unborn children carried by these mothers grew emotionally agitated (as indicated by increasingly rapid heartbeats) every time their mothers even *thought* of smoking. The mothers didn't have to actually smoke. Just the *idea* of smoking was enough to quicken the rhythm of the babies' hearts. By the third trimester, the unborn child had *learned to associate* the physiological signs that accompany thoughts of smoking with the discomfort that smoking actually produced for him in the womb.

Given such findings, it's more important than ever to communicate with your unborn child in a positive, loving fashion through touch, vision, and sound. Because your unborn child has increasingly advanced perceptual capabilities, however, this is also a good time to introduce some advanced techniques.

In "Rocking Your Baby" (Exercise 34), you will communicate with your unborn child through the rhythm of your breath and the rocking motion of your body. And in the third massage dialogue, "Massaging Baby Head to Toe" (Exercise 35), you will soothe your unborn child with a gentle but thorough massage.

Since your baby is now receptive to your inner emotional state, Month Seven is a good time to communicate with him sympathetically, through thought alone. You may find it particularly pleasurable to conduct "silent conversations" while listening to music or while immersed in the state of alert progressive relaxation. You may want to adapt "Small Talk," presented in Month Five, so that conversations with baby are sometimes nonverbal, taking place in a psychological or spiritual realm.

One of the most powerful ways to communicate with the unborn child sympathetically is through your dreams. The most potent dream technique for such communication, moreover, is *lucid dreaming,* in which you are aware of the fact that you're dreaming while in the midst of the dream. Following the techniques in Exercise 38, "Reaching Your Baby Through Lucid Dreams," you will recognize your dreams and attempt to communicate with your unborn child while in the dream state. Using this technique, you will explore your relationship with your baby, communicating your hopes and perhaps even trading places with your unborn child for a minute or two in your dreams.

By now, of course, you are an experienced dream worker. Recalling and recording your dreams each day, you are sure to notice when symbols and scenarios change. While dream symbols certainly mean different things to different people, the experts say that third-trimester dreams tend to reflect the growing baby and the impending birth. Patricia Maybruck, for instance, has found that in the later part of pregnancy, the unborn child may be symbolized by large animals, plants, or buildings. You might see the birth canal as a tunnel or a maze. As the birth date nears, the amniotic fluid may be represented by swimming pools, lakes, or oceans. Waves might represent the rise and fall of contractions. Scenes of death or natural disaster often indicate apprehension about giving birth.

During the third trimester, you may have more anxiety-ridden dreams. We suggest that you pay special attention to these dreams, and that you attempt to resolve the conflicts they reveal. By understanding your inner fears now, you will be better equipped to deal with the experience of giving birth. If highly disturbing dreams or nightmares disrupt your life and erode your sense of well-being, we suggest that you seek professional help.

As your baby's birth draws closer, you may find yourself more irritable and out of sorts, not just in dreams but in waking life as well. To enhance your feeling of health and energy, we suggest that you tap the "Feast on a Star" exercise introduced in Month Two. To help you gain a feeling of strength and energy, maintain wellness, and fight off disease, you can also turn to "Your Inner Healer" (Exercise 36). Based on an ancient—and very effective—visualization technique, the exercise will help you seek out the image of an inner healer or guide. With the help of this guide, you will visit a soothing, internal realm, marshaling the healing powers hidden in the farthest reaches of yourself. (The technique will help you boost your own immune system, as well as that of the child within.)

During Month Seven your baby will continue to grow and wake up to the world. It is therefore important that you talk to, sing to, and dance with your child. Continue to communicate through creative daydreaming, visualization, and massage as well. It is especially important that you practice alert progressive relaxation on a regular basis, and that you stay in touch with your emotions through dream work, journal writing (including right-brain writing), and dialogues with your spouse.

HELPING YOUR MATE RELATE TO YOUR UNBORN CHILD

There are millions of men who talk to, sing to, and play with their unborn children. These fathers frequently attend prenatal classes, massage their pregnant wives, and help throughout the birth.

Despite this trend, men usually have more difficulty relating to babies and infants than do women. A few men find it hard to communicate with their unborn children. If your husband is one of these men, it would be counterproductive to criticise him for it. Rather than getting into a hassle or dropping the subject altogether, talk to him about the research that supports the importance of communication with unborn children. Also discuss your need for him to take a more active role in your pregnancy. Finally, point out that relating to the baby is a two-way process, and parents can grow emotionally through their involvement with their children.

You might tell your spouse about the experience of a reporter from San Francisco. During her first pregnancy, her husband was a medical student and was hardly ever home. He even missed the birth of their baby. Several years later, when she became pregnant again, he spent every night at home. Each evening before going to sleep he would talk to the baby—about the weather, about what they'd had for dinner, and other simple things. He always concluded by telling the baby, "I love you and I look forward to seeing you soon."

When the baby was born, the father was present. As

soon as he got to hold his newborn son, the father started talking to him. The baby opened his eyes, looked at him intensely, and then smiled.

The reporter said she had no doubt whatsoever that this child recognized his father at once. She also commented that the relationship between the father and this second child was always stronger than that of the father to the first. She is certain that this is due to the prenatal bonding that took place with the second boy but not the first.

Exercise 34: Rocking Your Baby

THEME: Relaxing and deepening your psychological connection to your unborn child
INSTRUMENTS: Visualization and rhythmic breathing
PARTICIPANT: Mother
TEMPO: 30 minutes, once a week, for the rest of the month

The yogis of the East have made breathing a science, developing each particular breathing pattern to achieve goals in physical, emotional, and spiritual realms. With the help of rhythmic breathing, in fact, some yogis can perform seemingly miraculous feats, from voluntary regulation of heart rate and body temperature to increased tolerance of hunger and pain.

Western science has now confirmed that breathing in a rhythmic, highly regular way improves the flow of oxygen to the blood. As a result, the whole body seems to work more efficiently. Using rhythmic breathing, you will find that your head is clearer and your mind sharper; that your lungs function more easily; and that nutrients reach your cells more rapidly.

In recent years, yoga experts have developed breathing exercises for pregnant women as well. A version of the excellent exercise below was first developed by yoga expert Sylvia Klein Olkin when a few pregnant women joined one of her classes at a local YMCA. We have adapted her technique for this book. If you practice our rhythmic breathing exercise on a regular basis, you should find it easier to relax and strengthen your bond with the unborn.

Special Note: Your baby may become more active as you practice this breathing exercise because the technique increases the oxygen concentration in your bloodstream—and, obviously, your baby's bloodstream, too.

Begin by sitting in a comfortable position, and make sure you have about a half hour to yourself. Start by holding your hand about six inches above your pregnant abdomen for three to five minutes. Look down at your abdomen and envision the baby within. Picture your unborn child's tiny body, from the ten tiny fingers and ten tiny toes to the large head to the legs, curled and snug. Imagine the delicate features of your child's tiny face. See his mouth opening and closing, and picture his eyelids moving in the warmth of the amniotic fluid all around.

After you have absorbed the image of your baby as deeply as possible in your mind's eye, stand up and place both your hands on your abdomen. Now, with the image of your baby in your mind, inhale as you move your abdomen forward. Now exhale and move your abdomen back. Repeat. And repeat again. As you repeat these instructions, you will find that you are actually rocking your baby forward and back.

Spend a few minutes practicing the exercise in just this

way. The focus should be not on perfecting your breathing technique but on bonding with your unborn child. Tune in as deeply as possible to the rocking motion of your abdomen, and to the feelings of the child within.

When you feel in tune with your unborn child, close your eyes and inhale through your nose. As you inhale, imagine that your body is a long wind tunnel and that your breath is whooshing softly through you to massage the child within. As you inhale through your nose and exhale through your mouth, embrace your child with the hands you have placed on your abdomen. Caress your unborn child with your hands as you rock him back and forth. Remember, inhale as you move your abdomen forward; exhale as you move it back. As you continue the exercise in this way, notice that it should take about five seconds to inhale and five seconds to exhale. Feel the oxygen going into your nose, down into your lungs, then past your baby every time you breathe in. As you exhale —as you hug your baby—feel that same air coming back out.

Please practice this exercise until all the movements are fluid and even. The exercise will have a peaceful, almost hypnotic effect on you and will provide you with a deep sense of communion with the unborn.

Exercise 35: Massaging Baby Head to Toe

THEME: Tactile communication with the unborn
INSTRUMENTS: Movement, massage, and music or voice
PARTICIPANTS: Mother, father, and siblings
TEMPO: Ten minutes, twice a week, for the rest of the pregnancy

This exercise is similar to "First Massage Dialogue," presented during Month Six.

Whenever you feel your baby kick, stroke your abdomen as gently and lovingly as possible. Lie in a comfortable position that you can more or less maintain for about ten minutes. Then conduct the massage through a series of long broad strokes or through a series of sweeping circular motions. Last month, you stroked from below your belly button to below your breasts. This month, you should actually be able to feel the position of your baby's head and feet. Therefore, you will be able to stroke firmly and repetitively from his head toward his toes. Not only will this massage technique soothe and stimulate your unborn child, it will also add some depth and sparkle to the tactile language you used before.

As you have been doing all along, you may want to enhance this special period of communication by rubbing your abdomen with a light natural oil. As you massage your unborn child, you may want to play classical music, speak softly, or sing. Any of the songs or compositions recommended throughout the book would be appropriate. The important thing to remember is that every sound and movement should express your love. The gentle, consistent rhythm you create with your hands and your voice will help your baby feel confident and secure.

Special Note: If your partner or your other children decide to participate in this massage dialogue, we suggest that they also stroke the baby firmly and repetitively from head to toe, as opposed to using the more general massage technique outlined for Month Six.

Exercise 36: Your Inner Healer

THEME: Strengthening health and immunity for you and your unborn child
INSTRUMENTS: Alert progressive relaxation, visualization, guided imagery, and journal
PARTICIPANT: Mother
TEMPO: Thirty minutes, once a week, for the rest of the pregnancy

A persuasive body of scientific evidence now indicates that guided imagery and visualization can help to fight illness and disease. From such deadly maladies as cancer and heart disease to migraine headaches and allergies, visualization has proven a valuable supplement to conventional medical techniques.

Many experts also believe that visualization can help to promote wellness and boost your immunity, even when you are enjoying good health. Health, after all, is a continuum, with premature death and disability at one end and high levels of wellness at the other. If you are sick, visualization can help you get well; if you are already well, it can help you reach ever greater levels of immunity, vitality, and fitness.

Before you begin, record the instructions below on your tape recorder. We suggest that you recruit your partner or a close friend to read the words into your tape recorder for you; the voice of a trusted friend or lover is particularly effective. But if you prefer, you can record the instructions yourself. We suggest that the individual taping these instructions read them over silently before actually making the recording.

When ready, the reader should strive to read the script in a calm and relaxed manner, pausing where indicated. After the instructions have been recorded, find a comfortable chair and a footstool or ottoman on which you can prop your feet. Before you play your guided imagery tape, make sure you have at least thirty minutes to yourself. Before you turn on the tape recorder, close your eyes and, for just a few seconds, remember the sacred place you created and visited in Month Six. Also repeat this sentence to yourself: I will seek the guidance of my inner healer, who will help to enhance health and immunity for myself and my unborn child. *Your healer may take the form of a white-clad physician with tie and moustache, your intrepid great-grandmother, or a yogi from India. The exact form of your healer doesn't much matter as long as he or she embodies your own ability to explore—and enhance—your inner psyche and your health.*

Once you have completed these steps, open your eyes long enough to turn on your tape recorder and begin.

> *Close your eyes and take a couple of deep breaths. Continue to breathe deeply and evenly, allowing yourself to focus on the rhythm of your breathing, on your bodily sensations, and on any feelings and images about yourself. If thoughts about the outside world intrude upon you, just let them pass the way clouds pass over the horizon. Notice them, and then let them go.*
>
> *Now become aware of your feet. How do they feel pressed against the footstool or ottoman? Notice the pressure on them, and the angle at which they are placed. Become aware of the soles of your feet. Notice your heels, your toes, your ankles. Now begin to curl your toes toward the soles of your feet, as if*

trying to make contact. Push your toes down, down, down. Hold them and then let go.

Breathe in and out. Relax and let go.

With each breath that you take you are choosing to go deeper and deeper into a perfect state of relaxation. You are not falling asleep. You remain alert but relaxed.

Now become aware of your legs, from your knees down to your ankles. As you become aware of your legs, tighten all your leg muscles. Tighten, tighten, tighten. Hold. And relax.

Breathe in and out. Relax and let go.

With each breath that you take you are going deeper and deeper into yourself and your body is becoming more and more relaxed.

Now focus your attention on the middle of your body—your thighs, your pelvis, and your buttocks. As you become aware, tighten all the muscles in these areas. Tighten, tighten, tighten. Hold. And relax.

Breathe in and out. Relax and let go.

Continue to breathe deeply and evenly. With each inhalation, you are breathing in fresh oxygen and fresh energy. With each exhalation, you are breathing out carbon dioxide and bodily wastes. Think of each inhalation as a way of taking in love and support from the universe. Think of each exhalation as a means of ejecting negative feelings and tension.

Now become aware of your spine from your pelvis to the base of your head. Begin to press against the back of your chair or supporting cushions along the length of your spinal column. Push, push, push.

Now hold that position. And let go. Feel your back and your chest going limp.

Breathe in and out. Relax and let go.

Each breath that you take helps your body to relax. Whenever you inhale, every muscle—each individual cell—is nourished and energized. Whenever you exhale, every muscle—each individual cell—is cleansed of impurities and tensions.

Now become aware of your shoulders and your neck and all the tension that you store there. Begin to wash out this tension by pushing the tips of your shoulders up toward your ears; push until you feel as if you can almost touch your ears with your shoulders.

Push, push, push. Hold it. And let go.

Breathe in and out. Relax and let go.

Now lift your hands a few inches above your body and make a fist. Tighten your fist. Tighten, tighten, tighten. Hold. And let go.

Breathe in and out. Relax and let go. Continue to breathe deeply and evenly. With each breath that you take, you choose to become more relaxed. You feel comfortable and safe and secure.

Now become aware of your face. Notice the muscles around your eyes, your mouth, and your jaw. Squint your eyes. Tighten the muscles around your mouth. And tighten your jaw. Tighten, tighten, tighten. Hold. And let go.

Breathe in and out. Relax and let go.

Now that your body is relaxed, your mind should be relaxed as well.

In this relaxed but alert state of mind, seek out your sacred place, the peaceful internal sanctuary you visited in the past. As you did before, imagine your journey over geographical terrain to this private, peaceful realm. Now see your sacred place in detail. Whatever your sacred place, envision yourself there now.

[PAUSE FOR ONE MINUTE.]

Now look around for your inner healer. Search and wait for the embodiment of your inner healer to appear. If no inner healer emerges, walk around the grounds of your sacred place, exploring the environment until you find the person you seek. Take some time to observe the figure carefully, and ask his or her name. Accept whatever name comes to mind.

[PAUSE FOR THIRTY SECONDS.]

Now take your inner healer's hand and follow as he or she leads you from your sacred place to the shores of a warm ocean. Look around and see the subtle hues of the sand and water. Look up and watch the sea gulls flying gracefully overhead. Look all around and feel the healing rays of the sun. Take off your clothes and immerse yourself in the water. Sit on the soft bank of the sand near the shore, throw your head back, and open your arms and legs wide. Let the healing minerals of the water and the healing rays of the sun wash over you and enter the very core of your being. See the healing waters and the sunlight travel through every pore and channel of your inner being—through your heart and lungs, through your kidneys and liver, through all your cells. See the healing waters and sunlight travel through your abdomen, umbilical cord and placenta to every pore and channel of your unborn child. Watch as the healing light and water wash over your baby's tiny arms and legs, over his beautiful face and abdomen and through his inner organs—through his heart and lungs, through his kidneys and liver, through every one of his cells.

Stay with this image for about five minutes.

[PAUSE FOR FIVE MINUTES.]

If you have a specific problem, ask your inner healer to help you deal with it. If your pelvic muscles ache or feel weak, envision your healer rubbing a magical, healing salve over the region. If you feel generally tired, see your inner healer direct a revitalizing ray of light through your entire body. If you feel terrific, ask your inner healer to help you promote wellness for you and the child within. Do not consciously alter the images that come to mind —instead, simply ask your healer if he or she can tell you what you need to know. Do not stop to analyze the images that flow through your mind now. Simply watch them unfold, as they would in a film.

[PAUSE FOR TWO MINUTES.]

Now it is time for your inner journey to end. Follow your inner healer back to the peaceful realm of your sacred place. Take leave of your healer and, when you are ready, return to the present time and place.

[PAUSE FOR ONE MINUTE.]

Now slowly return to a state of complete waking consciousness. First wiggle your fingers and toes. Open your eyes. Remember to preserve your new sense of enhanced immunity, health, vitality, and calm. Still relaxed, use all your senses from vision to hearing to touch to focus on your immediate surroundings. Now, refreshed, revitalized, and relaxed, you may get up and continue with your day. As you go about your business, however, carefully consider the advice your inner healer has offered. If the advice makes sense to you, your partner, and your medical caregiver, consider incorporating it into your daily routine.

Special Note: The exercise above is not meant to replace conventional medical care. If your pregnancy is a healthy one, we suggest that you use our guided-imagery exercise to *supplement*—not to *replace*—your doctor's care. If your pregnancy is characterized by serious problems, practice guided-imagery techniques only with the help of a guided-imagery professional, referred to you by your personal physician or a nearby teaching hospital, and in conjunction with all recommended medical treatments.

If you like, you may use right-brain writing and drawing techniques to explore your feelings about the creative visualization exercise above. Keep up regular work with your journal.

Exercise 37: Orchestrating Birth

THEME: Having the kind of labor and delivery you want
INSTRUMENTS: Visualization and journal
PARTICIPANTS: Mother and father
TEMPO: Twenty minutes, once this month

Month Seven is a good time to consider whether the birthing environment you have chosen is truly right for you. We suggest that you practice the visualization part of the exercise while you are in the state of alert progressive relaxation so that you are especially attuned to your innermost feelings and thoughts. Please have your journal and pen or pencil by your side before you begin.

The first step of this exercise is to visit the actual place in which you will give birth, if you have not already done so. When you conduct your visit, explore the environment to your satisfaction and ask as many questions as you can.

At some point within twenty-four hours of the visit, find a comfortable place to sit and enter a state of alert progressive relaxation. You may use "Quick into the Deep" (Exercise 23), described in Month Five. Once you are deeply relaxed, picture, in your mind's eye, the environment in which you have decided to give birth. See the physical surroundings in as much detail as possible. Recall the people with whom you spoke and the questions that you asked. Now, while still deeply relaxed, ask yourself whether you feel good about giving birth in this environment. If you feel like it, you may even imagine the experience of going into labor, arriving at your birthing location, and ultimately giving birth at this locale. After you have envisioned your birth environment to your satisfaction, wiggle your fingers and toes, open your eyes, and assume a state of complete waking consciousness.

Once you are completely alert, take your journal and write down the following questions. Then, make sure you answer each one:

- *Will I be the center of my childbearing experience in the birthing place I have chosen?*
- *Will I be in charge of my childbearing experience in the birthing place I have chosen?*
- *Will I receive prompt and superior care in case of a medical emergency in the birthing place I have chosen?*
- *Will I receive the emotional support I deserve in the birthing place I have chosen?*
- *Do I have any doubts not covered by the questions above?*

Write all your feelings in your journal. If you like, you may use right-brain writing and drawing techniques to explore your feelings as well. When you are finished, analyze your thoughts and feelings and discuss them with your partner. If you feel that the birthing place you have chosen has too many negatives, consider exploring other alternatives. It is hard to find a birthing location that is perfect. But if the environment in which you have planned to have your baby seems seriously flawed, then now is the time to investigate other alternatives.

Exercise 38: Reaching Your Baby Through Lucid Dreams

THEME: Consciously seeking out your unborn child in your dreams
INSTRUMENTS: Dream work, visualization, and journal
PARTICIPANT: Mother
TEMPO: Three days in a row this month, then as often as you like for the rest of the pregnancy

Lucid dreams are dreams in which you are consciously aware of the fact that you are dreaming even while you are in the midst of the dream. Once you have achieved lucidity, you can often control your dreams much as a director controls a film or play. People exploring this frontier of consciousness have used lucid dreams to fly like Superman, create dream adventures, and solve problems in life and work. During pregnancy, you may use the lucid dream for these purposes as well. If you would like to do so, we suggest the book *Lucid Dreams in Thirty Days: The Creative Sleep Program,* by Keith Harary, Ph.D., and Pamela Weintraub (see Resource Guide). For the purposes of the Womb Harmonics System, we have adapted the creative sleep techniques for an exercise that will enhance your ability to communicate with the unborn.

Begin this exercise as soon as you wake up in the morning. Today, and for the next two days, ask yourself whether you are dreaming every so often from the time you get out of bed to the time you go to sleep. As you drive to work, as you go shopping or pick up your child from school, look around and say to yourself: Is this reality, or is this a dream? *After you pose the question, study the scene around you. Do the trees have ordinary brown bark and green leaves? Or are they rainbow-colored, with darting eyes? Is the sky the usual baby blue? Or is it silver and gold? What about that billboard on the city bus? Do the words and pictures change from one second to the next? Or do they remain consistently the same?*

Of course, most of the time, you will find the images in front of you consistent with reality. But every once in a while you will see an image that seems to be in direct conflict with the world as you know it. This is a signal that you are in the midst of a dream. If you happen to recognize that you are dreaming, say to yourself: I am dreaming. *(Please remember, however, that if you are driving a car, caring for a young child, or performing any other activity where attention to detail is crucial, you must carry on as usual even if you suspect you are dreaming.)*

Each night before you go to bed, repeat these words to yourself: Tonight I will recognize that I am dreaming while in the midst of a dream. When I recognize that I am dreaming, I will attempt to find my unborn child and establish communication.

Write these sentences in your dream journal, and, as you focus on the words you have just written, allow yourself to drift off to sleep.

If you are lucky, the techniques above will enable you to have lucid dreams. If not, you may wish to add the following step in the middle of the night, after you have awakened spontaneously from an ordinary, nonlucid dream. After you wake up from such a dream, lie quietly in bed without moving or opening your eyes. From the perspective of this nearly (but not completely) conscious state, think about the dream you just had. Then, using your visualization skills, review the dream in as much detail as possible. In the course of your visualization, pay attention to the setting, characters, plot, and overall imagery. Visualize the dream from beginning to end several times. Then go over the dream once more, this time adding two elements that were missing before: Imagine that you, the dreamer, are conscious of the dream states as the dream proceeds. Also imagine that at some point during the course of the dream you meet up with your unborn child. Now, repeat the two key phrases you wrote down just before falling asleep: Tonight I will recognize that I am dreaming while in the midst of a dream. When I recognize that I am dreaming, I will attempt to find my unborn child and establish communication. *Then allow yourself to drift off to sleep. You will probably find yourself rapidly descending from your nearly conscious state into a dream. Because you have been hovering somewhere between complete waking consciousness and dream sleep, however, you will be particularly suggestible. The result, after a bit of practice, may well be a lucid dream.*

Once you find yourself in a lucid dream, look around the dream terrain for your baby. If your baby is not immediately visible, walk, drive, or fly (yes, you can *fly like a bird in lucid dreams) until you have found your unborn child. Once you have found your baby, explore your relationship in the dream world. You may tell your child all you want for him, or ask him what he needs most. Since you are in control here, please remember to make the experience a positive one and to communicate your devotion and love.*

At some point in your lucid dream, you may even trade places with your unborn child. To do so, imagine how your dream experience would appear from the perspective of your unborn child. Then imagine yourself actually trading places with your baby and looking back—through your baby's eyes—at the dream character that, up until this point, has been you. Now that you have taken on the role of your unborn child in your dream, what do you feel like saying to the dream character who represents you? How do your feelings about yourself and your dream shift as you take on the viewpoint of your baby?

After you wake up, take your journal and describe any insights you may have gained from your lucid dream experience. If you like, express your feeling through right-brain writing or drawing as well.

Lucid dreaming is most effective when used sparingly. After all, dreams allow us to ventilate our emotions. If we are constantly controlling the action in our dreams, our deepest emotions may not find the expression they need. Therefore, we suggest that you do lucid dreaming only about once or twice a week, at most. If you find yourself having lucid dreams more often, simply watch the action without exerting active control.

Month Seven Summary

New Techniques

34. Rocking Your Baby	Rhythmic breathing to soothe yourself and your unborn baby	30 minutes, once a week
35. Massaging Baby Head to Toe	Communicating with your baby through massage	10 minutes, 2 to 5 times a week
36. Your Inner Healer	Promoting wellness	30 minutes, once a week
37. Orches-trating Birth	Exploring the birthing environment	20 minutes once this month

38. Reaching Your Baby Through Lucid Dreams	Communicating with your unborn baby through conscious dreams	3 days in a row this month

Familiar Techniques to Continue

1. Viva Vivaldi	Music to grow by	60 minutes, twice weekly
3. Daily Diary	Writing	Every day, as needed
4. Affirmations	Positive thinking	At least 2 minutes, twice daily
5. Dream Work	Understanding dreams	Every time you have a dream
7. Hello, Baby	Communicating with the baby	10–20 minutes, twice weekly
16. The Inner Circle	Harmonizing the mind	15 minutes, twice weekly
21. Moving Closer	Understanding your partner	30 minutes, weekly
23. Quick into the Deep (or Time Out for Mom)	Relaxation	Once or twice a day
24. Sweet Melodies	Singing to your baby	Every day
25. Story Time	Telling stories to the baby	Every day
26. Small Talk	Talking to your baby	Every day

28. Tiny Dancer	Sensing your baby's motion	Every day
29. Waltzing with Baby	Communicating with your baby through dance	10–20 minutes, twice weekly

Your Baby at Seven Months' Gestation

WEEK	SIZE AND WEIGHT	EMBRYOLOGICAL, FUNCTIONAL, AND PSYCHOLOGICAL CHANGES
28	13 in. (32 cm) 2 lbs (1 kg)	During this month the cerebral hemispheres expand enormously: six layers with large convolutions form. All the reflexes evident at birth, from sucking and rooting to grasping and stepping, are already present. When sweet, sour, or acrid substances reach your baby's tongue, he will respond by changing facial expression. If born at this point, your child would also react differently to different smells. At seven months' gestation, the unborn child not only moves in rhythm to music but actually shows preference for specific types of music. Twins, in fact, may react differently to the same piece of music while still in the womb. At this point in development, conditioned learning occurs: Your baby now signals displeasure through vigorous kicking and responds with consistent arm and leg movements to you and other family members when massaged through the abdominal wall.

You at Seven Months of Pregnancy

WEEK	THE PREGNANCY EXPERIENCE
26	The skin covering your pregnant abdomen becomes thin and begins to truly stretch. If you are going to have stretch marks, they will become obvious now. Indigestion and heartburn may begin to trouble you more than usual.
28	By now you may have gained more than nineteen pounds. A pound of that weight has been added just to your breasts.

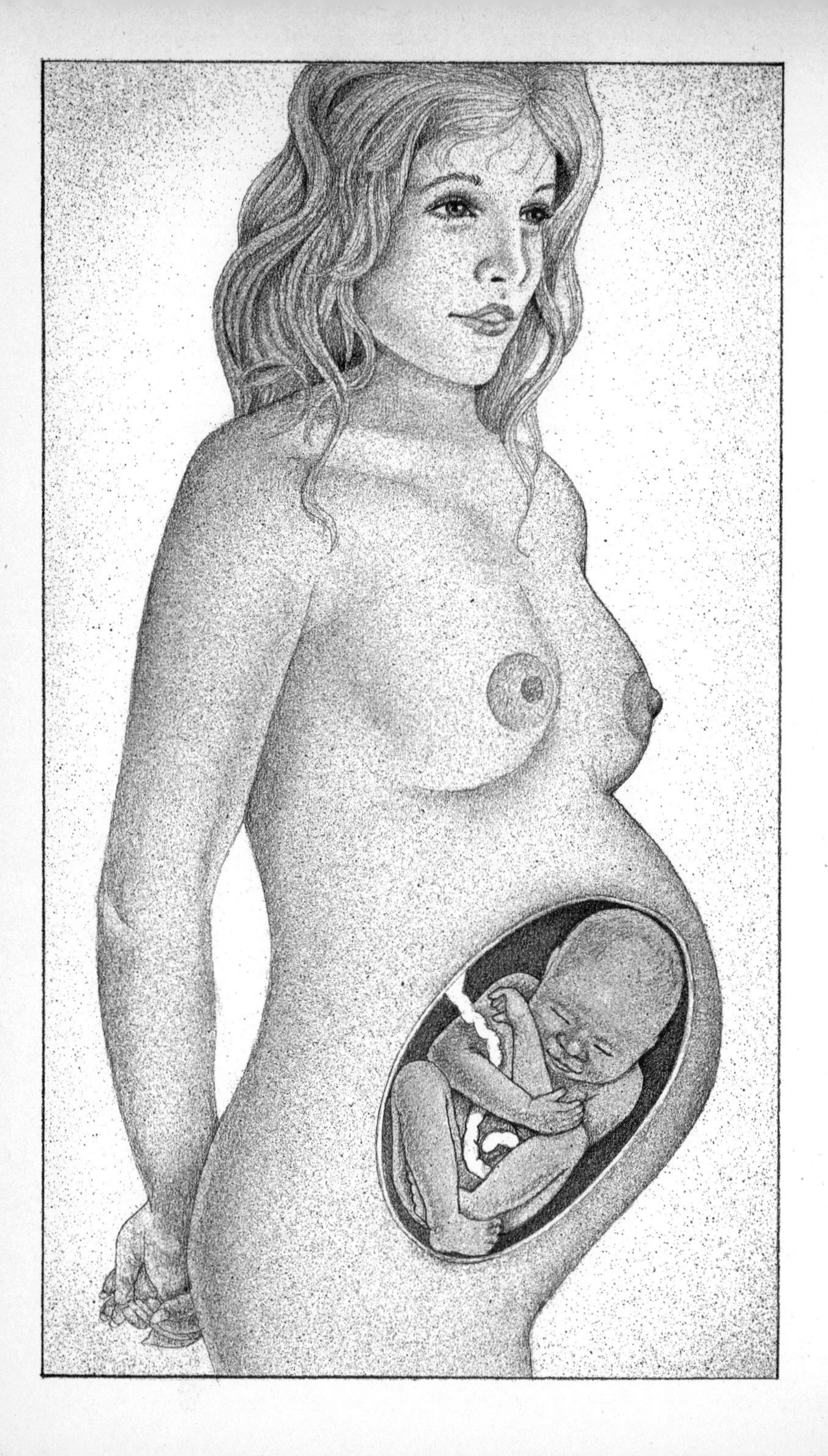

8

MONTH EIGHT: Awake in the Womb

By the eighth month of pregnancy, your baby has grown so large, and her movements have become so vigorous, that you can easily visualize her in your mind's eye. Your unborn child has become so responsive that she can react differently to the voices of you, your partner, siblings, and others. If she had to, your baby could now thrive outside the womb with relatively little difficulty.

Your baby's ever-increasing mental and physical capacity makes her particularly receptive to communications from the outside world. During Month Eight, in fact, you may actually play games with your unborn child. Through techniques suggested in "Play Time" (Exercise 39), you and your partner will learn to pat and tap your unborn child, eliciting a consistent, seemingly *conscious* response. You will also learn to communicate with your baby through the guttural, deeply emotional sounds you are likely to produce during labor.

Because labor may be just a few weeks away, we spend much of Month Eight helping you to prepare for labor and birth. Two guided-imagery exercises will help promote the dilation of your cervix and ease the passage of your baby through the birth canal. In "Releasing Birth Fears" (Exercise 40), you will use the journal-writing and affirmation techniques to alleviate anxiety about the experience of labor by dealing with your fears head-on. In "Prebirth Duet" (Exercise 41), we help you and your partner face fear of the birth experience together.

As in previous months, remember during Month Eight to talk to, sing to, and dance with your baby. Continue reading the story or stories you introduced during Month Five, and as often as possible, try to communicate with your child through lucid dreams. Since you may be quite busy with many of the Womb Harmonics exercises at this point, we suggest that when you enter the state of alert progressive relaxation each day, you do so with the help of the five-minute "Quick into the Deep" exercise presented in Month Five.

At this point, it may be useful for you to read the rest of the book. If you come across any exercises that you would like to incorporate into your present program, do not hesitate to do so now. Your baby may not be aware of our nine-month program and decide to surprise you with an early arrival!

Exercise 39: Play Time

THEME: Communicating with your baby through touch and play
INSTRUMENTS: Touch, movement, and play
PARTICIPANTS: Mother, father, and unborn child
TEMPO: A few minutes each day, whenever you like

During Months Eight and Nine of your pregnancy, you and your family can play with the unborn child. Push one finger into one side of the abdomen, then push another finger in on the other side. Do this a few times. The baby will, amazingly, respond. She may regularly move her hand or foot against her mother's fingers or kick every time she feels the mother, father, or other family member push into her domain.

You may also try patting the abdomen rhythmically, with two or even three beats together. You, like many other parents, may find that if you pat the abdomen twice, your baby will kick back twice in the exact location of the pat. If you pat the abdomen three times, your unborn child may kick back three times. Many mothers say that touching their babies hands through the abdominal wall for the first time is the most thrilling event of their pregnancy.

Exercise 40: Releasing Birth Fears

THEME: Overcoming fears about labor and delivery
INSTRUMENTS: Journal, affirmations, and visualization
PARTICIPANT: Mother
TEMPO: Thirty–forty-five minutes, once or twice this month

As pregnancy draws to a close, virtually all women worry about the rigors of labor and delivery. Some are able to cope with their worries, putting them in perspective so that the last trimester of pregnancy is a period of joy. Others dwell on their fears, generating a state of high anxiety for hours or days at a time.

High anxiety is an impediment not just to the health of your unborn child but to a problem-free labor and delivery as well. A University of Michigan study found that anxious women spent, on the average, many more hours in labor than calm women.

A University of Cincinnati study came up with similar results. In this study, researchers looked at ten different types of anxieties and stresses, and determined the effect each had on uterine contractions and labor time. The scientists found that extreme habitual worries and fears, a negative attitude toward motherhood, and a poor relationship with one's own mother prolonged labor most. Normal levels of anxiety, the study found, had very little impact on the efficiency of labor.

And in a study conducted by researchers at Brown University, the results were especially conclusive. Scientists there studied fifty women: Half of them were anxious about birth and motherhood, while the other half looked forward to birth and motherhood. After the women had delivered their babies, the researchers found that all the anxious women had at least one complication during delivery. In many instances, even their babies had difficulties, with problems ranging from a bruised nose to prematurity. As for the unworried mothers, their babies had no complications at all.

While a sense of calm won't guarantee a problem-free birth experience, it can certainly help. And the first step toward generating calm about labor and delivery is expressing your worries and fears.

Anxieties related to delivery include the fear of false labor, the fear of pain, and the fear of losing control during birth. Some women fear that their cervix won't dilate or that the baby may get stuck in the birth canal and simply not emerge. Women may fear the possibility of a forceps delivery, a cesarean delivery, or a baby whose presentation is breech.

Whatever *your* fears, you can best overcome them by admiting them to yourself and facing them head-on. Once you have examined your inner anxieties with the help of the exercise below, you will be able to put them in perspective and deal with them in a more productive fashion.

Sit in a comfortable spot with your journal during some quiet time of the day; make sure that for a period of thirty to forty-five minutes you will not be disturbed. Then close your eyes and ask yourself this question: What is it about the experience of childbirth that worries me most? *Let the answers pass through your mind for about five minutes, then open your eyes and start to write. Describe your fears with absolute honesty, writing anything that comes to mind. After you have finished, go back and read what you have written aloud. Read* slowly, *and allow the full impact of each fear to register in your mind. Then read the fear aloud again.*

Each time you pronounce a specific fear, try to turn the anxiety into a positive affirmation. For instance, if you fear that your baby will not be able to pass through your birth canal, say: My baby will pass through my birth canal smoothly and easily. *If you fear losing control during labor, say:* I will be conscious and competent from the beginning of my birth experience to the end. *Use the affirmations that work best for you, and create an affirmation in response to each and every fear.*

After you have said your affirmations aloud, write each one in your journal ten times in a row. When you have finished, softly caress your pregnant abdomen and, in your mind's eye, gaze right through it so that you see your baby floating in the amniotic sea. Then take leave of your baby and slowly get up and continue with your day.

If you like, you may repeat this exercise once more in the course of your last trimester. But don't dwell on your fears. After you have dealt with them in the straightforward manner outlined above, it is best that you release them and, thus unburdened, go on to bathe your unborn child with warmth and love.

Exercise 41: Prebirth Duet

THEME: Overcoming fears about labor and delivery
INSTRUMENT: Partner dialogue
PARTICIPANTS: Mother and father
TEMPO: Thirty–forty-five minutes once this month

It is important that you and your partner discuss your fears about the birth experience with each other. Therefore, we suggest that you use the following exercise during one of your regular partner dialogues this month.

As you do during every partner dialogue, sit facing each other. The task ahead is for both of you to share and shed your fears about birth. Remember the ground rules for all *partner dialogues: Tell the truth; speak from the heart; share your feelings; really* listen *to what your spouse is saying; be supportive; do not interrupt; do not make your partner feel guilty for what he is saying; and try to avoid feelings of guilt within yourself. Remember, while sharing feelings, to look into your partner's eyes. If you feel shy or embarrassed, just remind yourself that this exercise will help you cope once labor begins.*

Now you may begin. Start by looking at your partner and

completing the following sentence: "A fear I have about giving birth is ——."

Now your partner may reply with the following phrase: "Thank you for telling me that."

Now your turn: "Another fear I have about giving birth is ——."

Your partner's reply: "Thank you for telling me that."

Continue in this fashion until you have expressed all your fears and anxieties. Then switch roles and allow your partner to describe his fears about the upcoming birth as well. You must both repeat the exercise until you have nothing left to say.

If you wish, you may both then turn the fears you expressed into positive affirmations.

After you and your partner have dealt with your fears about birth, prepare yourself for the experience with the help of the next three exercises.

Exercise 42: The Pleasure Sigh

THEME: Rhythmic breathing and sighing to help you prepare for labor and communicate with the unborn
INSTRUMENTS: Visualization and rhythmic breathing
PARTICIPANT: Mother
TEMPO: Thirty minutes, at least once a week, for the rest of the pregnancy

Like "Rocking Your Baby" (Exercise 34) from Month Seven, "The Pleasure Sigh" is based on the pioneering work of yoga expert Sylvia Klein Olkin. The exercise below, in fact, builds on "Rocking Your Baby," but this time you will emit a long, loud *aahhhhh!* after each exhalation.

The sighing sound is a means of communicating with your unborn child. According to Olkin, "Making sounds helps the body to open up during labor." Practicing these guttural sounds during pregnancy, she notes, makes it easier to produce them during labor itself.

Before you begin, make sure that you are sitting in a comfortable position, and that you have about a half hour to yourself. Spend three to five minutes just holding your hand about six inches above your pregnant abdomen. Look down at your abdomen, envisioning the baby within. Picture your unborn child's tiny body, from the ten tiny fingers and ten tiny toes to the large head to the legs, curled and snug. Envision the delicate features of your child's tiny face. See her mouth opening and closing, and picture her eyelids fluttering in the warmth of the amniotic fluid all around.

After you have absorbed the image of your baby as deeply as possible, stand up and place both your hands on your abdomen. Now, with the image of your baby in your mind, inhale as you move your abdomen forward. Exhale, and move your abdomen back. As you exhale, open your mouth and let out a loud, long, guttural Aaaahh! *Repeat. And repeat again.*

After you feel in tune with your own rhythms and those of your unborn child, close your eyes and start inhaling through your nose. As you inhale, move your abdomen forward; at the same time, imagine that your body is a long wind tunnel, and that your breath is whooshing softly through you to massage the child within. As you exhale, move your abdomen back; at the same time, open your mouth and let out a loud, long, guttural Aaaahh! *As you breathe and sigh, rock your child back and forth and embrace her with your hands. Remem-*

ber, inhale as you move your abdomen forward; exhale and sigh as you move your abdomen back. As you continue the exercise in this way, it should take about five seconds to inhale and five seconds to exhale and sigh. Feel the oxygen going into your nose, down into your lungs, and then past your baby every time you breathe in. As you sigh and exhale—as you hug your baby—feel that same air coming back out.

Practice this exercise until all the movements are fluid and even. The exercise will have a calming effect on you and will deepen your sense of communion with the unborn. It should also make it far easier for you to ventilate your feelings through long, guttural sighs as labor ensues.

Exercise 43: The Unfolding Flower

THEME: Preparing your cervix to open at birth
INSTRUMENT: Visualization
PARTICIPANT: Mother
TEMPO: Fifteen minutes, twice a week from now until birth

You have already used visualization to help you relax, boost your health and energy, get in touch with your inner emotions, and communicate with the unborn. Now you will use the technique to prime your body for labor and birth.

Visualization has been used to perfect athletic performance for decades. From Olympic skiers and skaters to quarterbacks and goalies, superstar athletes have marshaled enormous inner resources, ultimately achieving their full potential, by visualizing their events.

As anyone who has given birth knows, labor is one of the most athletic events many women may ever face. In Lamaze class, you are learning breathing techniques to help you through the rigors of this event. But visualization techniques are highly effective as well. With that in mind, practice "The Unfolding Flower" for 10 minutes twice a week throughout the rest of your pregnancy. You will prepare your cervix to open more easily when labor begins. If practiced on a regular basis, this exercise will prime your body on the deepest level, literally helping your muscles rehearse some of the movements they will make during the actual event.

Before you begin, make sure that you are sitting in a comfortable position and that you have about fifteen minutes to yourself. If possible, dim the lights or draw the shade. Now use the "Quick into the Deep" technique (Exercise 23) to induce the state of alert progressive relaxation.

After you have entered the state of alert progressive relaxation, imagine yourself walking in a garden with hundreds of flowers. Look around, and choose a flower you find yourself attracted to. Take your time. The red rose, the white lily, the yellow daffodil, or any other petaled flower will do. Take the flower in your hand. Now imagine it opening, slowly, very slowly, one petal at a time. Picture it opening wider and wider until it is fully open to the world.

Spend about five minutes on this visualization, adding whatever details make it most real for you. See the precise color of the flower, the dewdrops on its leaves, the grains of pollen within. Smell the flower's fragrance; hear the singing of a nearby bird or the buzzing of a bee.

After you have spent about five minutes envisioning your unfolding flower, look down at your pelvis. Imagine the flower with its petals closed and superimposed over your pel-

vis. Then imagine the flower—and your cervical muscles—opening, slowly, very slowly, a little at a time. Feel the muscles in your pelvic region tingle. Let the image linger for about five minutes until, in your mind's eye, the flower and your cervix are fully open.

After you have envisioned the flower—and your cervix—unfolding, picture them closing again. Remind yourself that when it's time to give birth to your baby, your cervix will gradually open just as the flower opens when the sun rises at the start of the day. Remind yourself that after your baby has passed through the birth canal, your cervix will close just as the flower closes with the setting sun. It is the most natural process in the world. Nature has been practicing this art for millions of years. Trust your body. Now wiggle your fingers and toes, open your eyes, and assume a state of complete waking consciousness.

Special Note: During actual labor, use "The Unfolding Flower" exercise repeatedly to help you dilate your cervix.

Exercise 44: The Whispering Flute

THEME: Preparing your birth canal for the baby
INSTRUMENT: Rhythmic breathing and visualization
PARTICIPANT: Mother
TEMPO: Ten minutes, once a week, from now until birth

Before you begin, make sure that you are sitting in a comfortable position and that you have about ten minutes to yourself. Place both your hands on your abdomen and spread your legs apart. Now, inhale and exhale through your mouth.

(Inhalation and exhalation should take around five seconds each.) Continue breathing in and out through your mouth, in and out, more and more deeply. Repeat, and repeat again.

As you breathe in, imagine within your body a long flute connecting your mouth to your vagina. Play this imaginary flute: Inhale and blow air down the tube past your baby in the womb, past your cervix, and out through your vagina. As air moves down the body of the flute, feel all the surrounding tissues and muscles becoming increasingly relaxed, until they feel very open, very loose, very ready for birth. Breathe in again, and again blow the air into your flute. Repeat the process until you have created a wide-open passageway for birth. As you become more familiar with this technique, try to actually play a melody on your flute. Use your imagination and have fun.

After you have played your whispering flute for about ten minutes, go on with the rest of your day.

Special Note: Use this breathing and visualization exercise as you push your baby through the birth canal. You will be surprised at how helpful "The Whispering Flute" may be in easing the passage for you and your soon-to-be born.

Month Eight Summary

New Techniques

39. Play Time	Playing with the unborn	2–5 minutes, as often as you like
40. Releasing Birth Fears	Overcoming anxiety about birth	30–45 minutes, once or twice this month
41. Prebirth Duet	Sharing feelings about labor and delivery with your partner	30–45 minutes, once this month

42. The Pleasure Sigh	Using breathing and sound to communicate with your baby and prepare for labor	30 minutes, once a week for the rest of the pregnancy
43. The Unfolding Flower	Preparing your cervix for birth	15 minutes, twice a week
44. The Whispering Flute	Preparing your birth canal for birth	10 minutes, once a week

Familiar Techniques to Continue

1. Viva Vivaldi	Music to grow by	60 minutes, twice weekly
3. Daily Diary	Writing	Every day, as needed
4. Affirmations	Positive thinking	At least 2 minutes, twice daily
5. Dream Work	Understanding dreams	Every time you have a dream
16. The Inner Circle	Harmonizing the mind	15 minutes, twice weekly
23. Quick into the Deep (or Time Out for Mom)	Relaxation	Once or twice a day
24. Sweet Melodies	Singing to the unborn	Every day
25. Story Time	Telling stories to your baby	Every day
26. Small Talk	Talking to your baby	Every day
28. Tiny Dancer	Sensing your baby's motion	Every day

You have by now worked with many techniques. Please keep up with those you feel are most useful. Do not feel you must keep up with every single exercise on the list above. Remember, the goal here is to reduce stress, not increase it.

Your Baby at Eight Months' Gestation

WEEK	SIZE AND WEIGHT	EMBRYOLOGICAL, FUNCTIONAL, AND PSYCHOLOGICAL CHANGES
32	14 in. (38.0 cm) in the sitting position 4–5 lbs (2–2.5 kg)	Your baby has gained about two pounds in the past month; most of the weight gain consists of fat deposited under the skin. The eyelids are no longer fused. Eyebrows and head hair appear. Skin functions efficiently to protect your baby against heat loss. During this month, the right and left hemispheres of the brain begin working together. Your unborn child reacts differently to voices of mother, father, and unknown people. If born now, your baby would survive with relative ease outside the womb.

You at Eight Months of Pregnancy

WEEK	THE PREGNANCY EXPERIENCE
30	You once more feel quite tired, perhaps even exhausted. If you exert yourself too much, you may even feel breathless. If you look down at your abdomen, your navel looks flat, and the dark line known as the linea negra is clearly seen running down your abdomen.
32	Your ribs may begin to spread out to accommodate your rapidly enlarging uterus. You may experience backache and general discomfort throughout much of your body. Your bladder may feel irritable and full, and you probably feel the need to urinate frequently. When your baby's head descends into your pelvic cavity, you should feel considerably more comfortable. Around this time, you may also notice an increase in Braxton-Hicks contractions, a painless, erratic relaxation and tightening of the uterus.

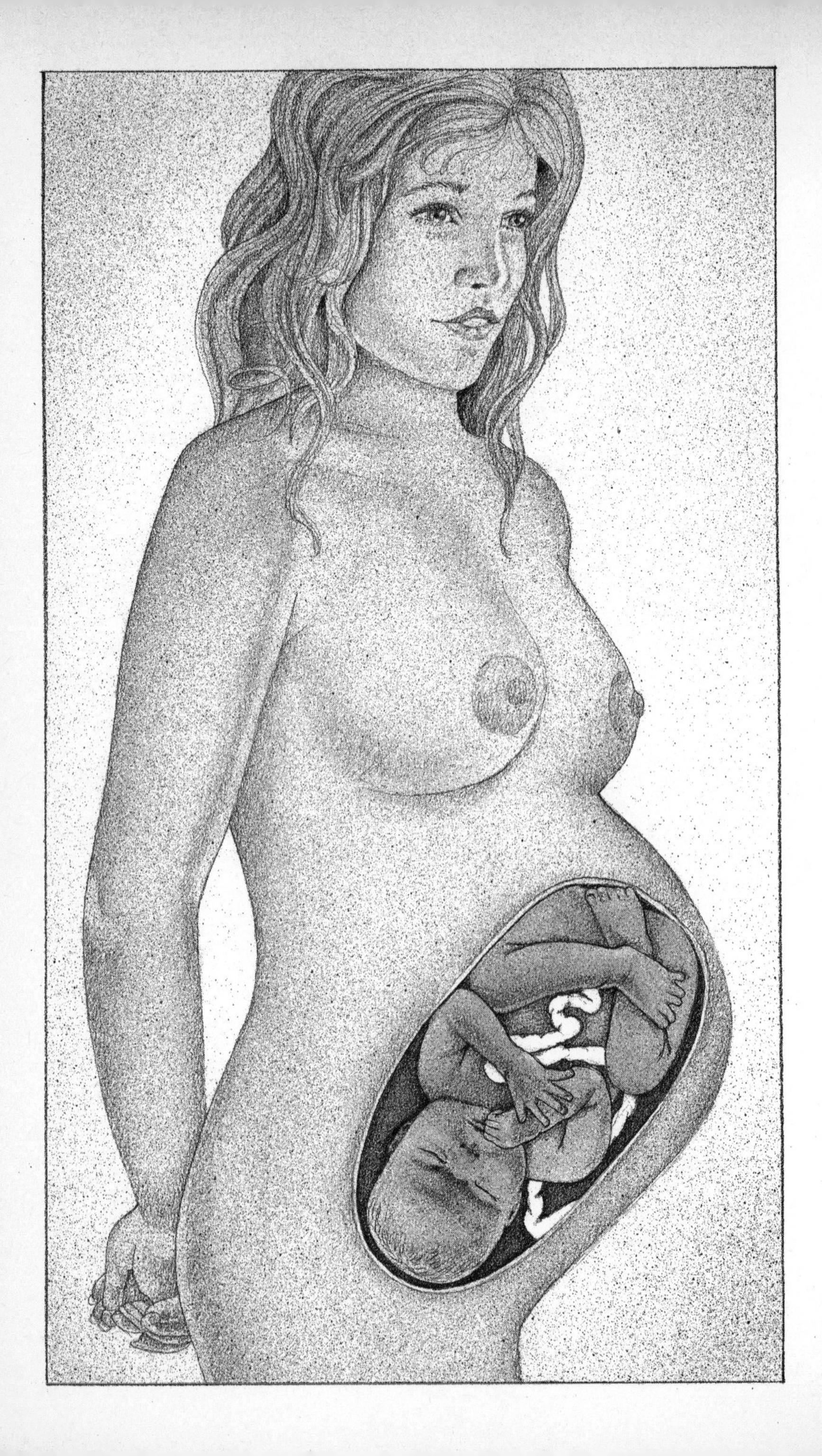

9

MONTH NINE:
Toward Emergence

You are now entering the ninth—and last—month of your pregnancy. During this month, your baby will acquire antibodies from your blood. He probably has some scalp hair, and his fingernails and toenails have grown so long they require trimming. By the end of this month, your baby will be fully developed. He will weigh about seven pounds, on average, and measure about twenty inches in length. He will, in short, be ready to be born.

We will devote Month Nine, therefore, to preparing you, your partner, and your baby for the momentous event of birth. In "The Warm Glow" (Exercise 45), we will help you relieve the tension sure to increase as the moment of labor approaches. In "Ready and Able" (Exercise 46), we present a series of powerful affirmations meant to help you develop full confidence in your ability to give birth.

In addition to working with the special Month Nine exercises, you should use this time to make some preparation for the baby about to be born. We do not recommend *elaborate* preparation, but you should take care of a few essentials that might be difficult to deal with immediately after birth. For instance, you should prepare some clothes in which you can take your baby home from the hospital or birthing center. Even if you do not want to acquire a whole wardrobe or baby furniture, this is a suitable time to order items to be delivered to your home *after* the birth. This is also a good time to investigate diaper services; to choose a pediatrician; to obtain information on breast feeding; and to discuss the pros and cons of circumcision with your partner. If you plan to return to work a few months after your baby is born, we also suggest that you investigate child-care options *now.*

To make sure that you keep track of all items you must see to before your baby is born, please make lists and take notes in your journal.

Finally, you might find this an opportune time to consider who you would like to attend the birth of your baby. If you are unsure about whether or not a particular person should be present, simply imagine the place you plan to give birth. Imagine the individual in question in this special environment, then ask yourself whether you truly want to share the birth experience with this person. Will this individual help to soothe and relax you? Will this person help to make the birth experience beautiful and meaningful? Will this person be a truly positive force at your baby's birth? Do not hesitate to add or subtract from the list of those who will comprise your birth party. Be true to your feelings and convictions.

Continue to tap the techniques that have proven the most useful and enriching, and remember to keep up with the exercises that prepare your cervix for birth. Also, continue to massage, sing to, and talk to your unborn child until the day he enters the world.

Exercise 45: The Warm Glow

THEME: Relieving tension and discomfort
INSTRUMENTS: Guided imagery
PARTICIPANT: Mother
TEMPO: Five minutes, as often as you like

Before you begin this exercise, record the instructions below on your tape recorder. As in other guided-imagery exercises, we suggest that you recruit your partner or a close friend to read the words into your tape recorder. But if you prefer, you can record the instructions yourself. We suggest that the individual taping these instructions read them over silently before actually making the recording. When ready, the reader should strive to read the script below slowly and calmly, pausing where indicated.

After the instructions have been recorded, find a comfortable chair and a footstool or ottoman on which you can prop your feet. Before you play your guided-imagery tape, make sure you have about five to ten minutes to yourself.

> *Imagine yourself lying in the sun, the golden rays of light bathing your skin and penetrating your body to wash over your unborn child, your inner organs, and your muscles and bones. Feel your entire being, inside and out, glowing with the sun's energy and warmth.*
>
> *Now breathe in and out, in and out, as deeply and fully as you can. Each time you breathe in, imagine yourself inhaling the gentle, glowing warmth of the sun. Imagine the sunlight drenching*

your inner body and the body of your unborn child with rays of energy and health. Imagine the light spreading out to fill every inch of your body. Imagine the light expanding and expanding until it surrounds you with a luminous, golden glow.

Now imagine the light growing particularly luminous, particularly bright, in any part of your body that feels tense or uncomfortable. Imagine the light pulsing and vibrating in that tense or uncomfortable region of your body until the pain or tension is totally dissolved.

Special Note: This exercise may help you deal with tension and discomfort during the last leg of your pregnancy, but it is also a valuable technique to use during labor itself.

Exercise 46: Ready and Able

THEME: Optimum labor and delivery
INSTRUMENTS: Affirmations and journal
PARTICIPANT: Mother
TEMPO: Five minutes, once a day, until birth

To begin, please read the following affirmations aloud, one by one.

- *I am fully able to cope with labor.*
- *I can labor in perfect harmony with nature.*
- *Childbirth is a normal, healthy event.*

- *I am creating a safe, healthy birth for myself and my baby.*
- *I am ready and able to have my baby now.*

After you have read through these affirmations, turn to an empty page in your journal and fold it in half. On the left-hand side of the page, write the first affirmation. For this affirmation (and all others in this exercise) include your own name in the statement. For instance, if your name is Michelle, you would write, I, Michelle, am fully able to cope with labor. *Make sure that as you print the statement, you* feel *its meaning as deeply as possible. You might also repeat the affirmation aloud. After you have printed the affirmation on the left, turn to the right-hand side of the page and record your reaction, whatever it may be. If you fear the affirmation may not be true, explain why. Take each affirmation through five to ten repetitions, until all your doubts and feelings have been expressed. As you write, notice the changes in your response from one repetition to the next. As you express your feelings, you will purge your negative thought-patterns, allowing positive thoughts and feelings to emerge.*

If there are other affirmations you would like to add to this list, please feel free to do so. The important thing is that you bolster your confidence about your ability to deal with the rigors of labor and delivery.

Month Nine Summary

New Techniques

45. The Warm Glow	Relieving tension and discomfort	5 minutes, when needed
46. Ready and Able	Affirming your ability to give birth	5 minutes, once daily

Familiar techniques to continue

1. Viva Vivaldi	Music to grow by	60 minutes, twice weekly
3. Daily Diary	Writing	Every day, as needed
4. Affirmations	Positive thinking	At least 2 minutes, twice daily
5. Dream Work	Understanding dreams	Every time you have a dream
16. The Inner Circle	Harmonizing the mind	15 minutes, twice weekly
23. Quick into the Deep (or Time Out for Mom)	Relaxation	Once or twice a day
24. Sweet Melodies	Singing to your baby	Every day
25. Story Time	Telling stories to your baby	Every day
26. Small Talk	Talking to your baby	Every day
28. Tiny Dancer	Sensing your baby's motion	Every day
39. Play Time	Playing with the unborn	2–5 minutes, as often as you like
43. The Unfolding Flower	Preparing your cervix for birth	15 minutes, twice a week
44. The Whispering Flute	Preparing your birth canal for birth	10 minutes, once a week

Your Baby at Nine Months' Gestation

WEEK	SIZE AND WEIGHT	EMBRYOLOGICAL, FUNCTIONAL, AND PSYCHOLOGICAL CHANGES
35	14–15 in. (35–37.5 cm) 6 lbs (3 kg)	Your baby's head may descend into the pelvic cavity at about this time, especially if this is your first pregnancy.
36–38	20 in. (52 cm) 7¼ lbs (3.5 kg)	Your baby assumes an upside-down position. His head descends into your pelvic cavity before labor begins. His fingernails and toenails are formed. He is less active because of cramped quarters. He is mentally ready to engage the world.

You at Nine Months of Pregnancy

WEEK	THE PREGNANCY EXPERIENCE
34	Your baby's movements decrease because of less space in the womb. But you still feel strong jabs and pushing movements from the hands and feet.
35–36	Your ribs may begin to spread out to accommodate your rapidly enlarging uterus. You may experience backache and general discomfort throughout much of your body. Your bladder may feel irritable and full, and you probably feel the need to urinate frequently. When your baby's head descends into your pelvic cavity, you should feel considerably more comfortable. Around this time, you may also notice an increase in Braxton-Hicks contractions.
38 (Term)	You discharge the mucous plug in your cervix with a small amount of blood. Your water may break. Contractions begin and increase in intensity and frequency. Labor begins.

10

GIVING BIRTH: Into the Light

We hope that your participation in the Womb Harmonics program has enabled you to plan an emotionally rewarding birth. For without a bit of planning, research, and forethought, you may lose some control over the birth experience.

Indeed, the last hundred years have seen labor and delivery move out of the home and into the hospital, where medically trained professionals may tend to view the birth experience in medical and surgical terms. Although medical professionals have the best of intentions, they often view the laboring woman as a patient, and a sick one at that.

From the time she enters the hospital, the pregnant woman must observe hospital rules. First, she is given a name tag with a number. Then she is asked to disrobe and change into a hospital gown. Confined to her room, she finds a never-ending stream of nurses, interns, and even residents continually probing and examining her. Because staff members are experts and she is not, the pregnant woman is made to feel as if others know more about her body than she does. Gradually, her sense of individuality, self-esteem, and self-control may erode. And though she may express her needs or inclinations clearly, well-intentioned medical professionals surrounding her may insist that her desires are less relevant than their own clinical opinions.

This stressful situation can obviously increase anxiety. And a high level of anxiety can interfere with the birth process by decreasing the efficiency of contractions and increasing muscular tension. More muscle tension will lead to more pain and more pain to more anxiety.

Fear and tension cause all of us to shift into a flight-or-fight pattern. One result of this innate physiological stress reaction is the shunting of blood from internal organs such as the uterus to the large muscles. This is a good system for someone running from a lion, but not so good for the woman giving birth. As blood rushes from the uterus, after all, it will flow away from the baby as well.

As the pain and anxiety increase, the hospital staff, attempting to be helpful, may offer the laboring woman painkillers. These medications, in turn, will slow down contractions. As contractions slow, the doctors themselves may become more anxious. They may then respond with such interventions as forceps, induction of labor with pitosin, or even cesarean section.

As you can see, it is easy for the modern childbirth experience to be stripped of its personal character. Rewards are diminished and a host of problems emerge.

We are not suggesting that you avoid hospitals and have your baby at home. Although that might be best from the psychological standpoint, studies show that home births are not as safe as hospital births. A good compromise is to give birth in a birthing center that is properly staffed and equipped for emergencies, or in a comfortable, quiet, and homelike birthing room in a hospital. Even if you have your baby in a more conventional hospital environment, you can, with proper planning, ensure a nurturing, positive emotional ambience in which to give birth.

The first step is finding an obstetrical staff with a "high-touch" instead of a "high-tech" orientation. These professionals must agree to use no fetal heart monitors, drugs, episiotomies, or forceps unless they are really necessary and you agree to them. Before you enter the hospital, make sure you will have the freedom to walk around throughout your labor and to give birth in any position you like. And of course, be certain that your spouse, your chosen birth attendant, and any other selected friends or family will be permitted to stay by your side throughout.

During labor and delivery, use as many of the Womb Harmonics techniques as you like. Make sure, for instance, that you remember to bring the prenatal music tape you prepared during pregnancy. Do not forget the three crucial visualization exercises: "The Unfolding Flower," "The Whispering Flute," and "The Warm Glow." And, if you begin to lose confidence in your ability to labor effectively, please tap the list of affirmations offered below. If possible, before you go to the hospital make sure that your birth attendants agree to dim the lights during labor, creating an atmosphere of unhurried calm. Also make sure they will place your baby on your chest *right after* birth. Also arrange for immediate father/baby contact *in advance.* Your spouse may hold the newborn and, if possible, even give the baby a bath.

If both you and your baby are healthy, we suggest that you share the same room following the birth. Whether or not you breastfeed, make sure that you touch, cuddle, and talk to your baby as much as possible during your stay in the hospital. Then go home with your baby as soon as you can. By the way, if you would like, sometime after you have left the hospital, you may want to take your special journal and describe the labor and delivery in as much detail as possible. Include a physical description of the labor and birthing rooms and record any conversations you can recall, particularly those conversations you had with your spouse. You may also wish to describe the way you reacted when you first saw, and then when you first held, your child. Also describe your baby's first few days, whether in the hospital or at home.

Exercise 47: Yes I Can

THEME: Boosting self-confidence during labor and delivery
INSTRUMENT: Affirmations
PARTICIPANT: Mother
TEMPO: As often as you like, throughout labor and delivery

Please use these special affirmations to help you deal with labor and delivery. To use them effectively, simply repeat any of the ones that seem helpful as often as you like.

- *I am laboring in perfect harmony with nature.*
- *I am ready and able to have my baby right now.*
- *The power of my contractions will carry my baby from the womb.*
- *I can push my baby into the world.*
- *My contractions are propelled by the laws of nature.*
- *My cervix will open like a blossoming flower, allowing my baby to emerge.*

Other Exercises to Use During Labor and Delivery

1. Viva Vivaldi	Music for concentration	Throughout labor
43. The Unfolding Flower	Helping your cervix dilate during birth	Throughout labor
44. The Whispering Flute	Helping your birth canal widen during birth	Throughout labor
45. The Warm Glow	Relieving tension and discomfort	Throughout labor

AFTERWORD

We hope that the forty-seven Womb Harmonics exercises have helped to make your pregnancy joyous and fulfilling. Our greatest wish for you, your partner, and your baby is that the love you have shared throughout the past nine months continues to flourish and grow. At *every* stage of development, even in adulthood, your child will need your love and acceptance, your deep commitment and involvement, and your willingness to communicate and share. For this reason, the skills you have learned during the past nine months should help your family grow happily together for years. Good luck! We wish all of you a wonderful, loving journey through life!

RESOURCE GUIDE

Books

Baker, Jeannine Parvati, Frederick Baker, and Tamara Slaytor. *Conscious Conception.*
Monroe, Utah: Freestone Publishing Co., 1986.

A rich and heady mixture of myth, metaphor, fantasy, art, poetry, and fact, this book reminds us of our roots in nature.

Baldwin, Rahima. *You Are Your Child's First Teacher.*
Berkeley, California: Celestial Arts, 1989.

Enhancing your child's development through age six.

Berends, Polly Berrien. *Whole Child/Whole Parent.*
New York: Perennial Library, 1987.

The one and only book about childrearing written by a mystic. Berends establishes, with exquisite accuracy, the connections between the hard-won wisdom of the best parents and the wisdom of the great sages of all times and cultures.

Chamberlain, David B., Ph.D. *Babies Remember Birth.*
Los Angeles, California: Jeremy P. Tarcher, 1988.

Chamberlain, an international leader in the new field of pre- and perinatal psychology, describes the amazing mind of the newborn, presenting scientific evidence for highly developed cognition and reason. He presents evidence for the theory that newborns are aware of their births and can recall them in detail when, as adults, they are hypnotized.

Chamberlain, David B., Ph.D. *Consciousness at Birth:* A Review of the Empirical Evidence.
San Diego, California: Chamberlain Communications, 1983.

Synthesizes research findings from a variety of sources and presents them clearly and concisely. A must for any serious student of pre- and perinatal psychology.

Cohen, Nancy Wainer, and Lois J. Estner. *Silent Knife.*
South Hadley, Massachusetts: Bergin & Garvey Publishers, 1983.

Provides a critique of this country's growing reliance on cesarean section and presents methods and strategies to prevent unnecessary cesareans. A good guide to natural childbirth.

Elliot, Role. *Mother and Baby Book.*
Glasgow, Scotland: William Collins, 1989.

Raising a baby on a healthy vegetarian diet.

Gardner, Joy. *Healing Yourself Through Pregnancy.*
Ann Arbor, Michigan: McNaughton, Gunn, 1987.

Offers herbal and natural cures for more than thirty common complaints of pregnancy. Also suggests ways to improve health for conception, foods to eat, and herbs to avoid during pregnancy, and many useful tips for nursing.

Grof, Stanislav. *Realms of the Human Unconscious.*
New York: E. P. Dutton, 1976.

No work so beautifully incorporates the findings of Freud, Jung, and Rank. Throws fresh light on the human perinatal experience and on death-rebirth symbolism as found in art, religion, and psychopathology. A modern classic, as relevant today as it was when first published.

Harary, Keith, and Pamela Weintraub. *Lucid Dreams in 30 Days: The Creative Sleep Program.*
New York: St. Martin's Press, 1989.

This handbook provides a step-by-step program for recalling, inducing, and ultimately controlling dreams.

Jones, Carl, with Jan Jones. *The Birth Partner's Handbook.*
New York: Meadowbrook Press, 1989.

This step-by-step guide shows the father, relative, or friend how to help a woman give birth, minimize her pain and maximize her joy.

Kagan, Jerome. *Unstable Ideas.*
Cambridge, Massachusetts: Harvard University Press, 1987.

This book is for the reader with a good grounding in developmental psychology. It explores such topics as malleability of temperament, milestones of cognitive development, the unconscious as a window onto the self, and the nature-nurture conundrum.

Kitzinger, Sheila. *The Complete Book of Pregnancy and Childbirth.*
New York: Alfred A. Knopf, 1989.

Fully revised and expanded, this book describes the development of the baby inside the uterus as well as the physical and psychological changes that occur throughout pregnancy. Includes a complete illustrated guide to labor, including the different forms of pain relief and the methods of delivery.

Kitzinger, Sheila. *Your Baby Your Way.*
New York: Pantheon Books, 1987.

Where should you have your baby? Through what method? Under whose care? What foods should you eat? What drugs should you avoid? These are some of the questions this refreshingly down-to-earth book answers.

Laing, R. D. *The Facts of Life.*
New York: Pantheon Books, 1976.

This book begins with autobiographical flashbacks to early childhood, then moves into questions and speculations about intra-uterine life and mythology, dreams and fantasies, reflections on birth and birth practices and many other areas of science and ethics. A thought-provoking and brilliant book, and a personal favorite.

Leboyer, Frederick. *Birth without Violence.*
New York: Alfred A. Knopf, 1976.

The book that started the obstetrical revolution, leading to a more gentle, human type of birth. Poetic and directed at both the heart and the mind of the reader.

Maybruck, Patricia, Ph.D. *Pregnancy and Dreams.*
Los Angeles; Jeremy P. Tarcher, 1989.

Describes the dreams and fantasies of pregnant women and discusses ways of understanding them.

Nilsson, Lennart. *A Child Is Born,* new edition.
New York: Delacorte Press, 1990.

Nilsson, a pioneer in the field of scientific medical photography, literally illuminates the mystery of human development from conception to birth. Enthusiastically recommended.

Noble, Elizabeth. *Having Twins.*
Boston: Houghton Mifflin, 1980.

The first complete guide for couples about to give birth to twins, triplets, or other multiples. Helpful hints from experienced parents cover the feeding, dressing, and raising of young twins.

Noble, Elizabeth. *Having Your Baby by Donor Insemination.*
Boston: Houghton Mifflin, 1987.

The most up-to-date and thorough analysis of the practical, legal, and ethical problems infertile couples face in becoming parents through third-party conception.

Olkin, Sylvia Klein. *Positive Pregnancy Fitness.*
Garden City, New York: Avery Publishing Group, 1987.

A catalogue of ideas for coping with the common discomforts of pregnancy. The author draws heavily on her knowledge of yoga, exercise, massage, shiatsu, nutrition, visualization, and other alternatives to mainstream medical care. Her love and respect for the unborn child permeate this excellent book.

Panuthos, Claudio. *Transformation through Birth.*
South Hadley, Massachusetts: Bergin & Garvey Publishers, 1984.

Provides a vision of birth that is whole and life-affirming. Panuthos helps women to grow through the experience of pregnancy and birth.

Peterson, Gayle. *Birthing Normally.*
Berkeley, California: Mindbody Press, 1984.

A practical guide to understanding and applying holistic principles of prenatal care for the physician, midwife, and childbirth educator interested in decreasing complications of birth. The relaxation and visualization exercises are especially recommended.

Ray, Sondra, and Bob Mandel. *Birth and Relationships.*
Berkeley, California: Celestial Arts, 1987.

Two leading voices in the international rebirthing movement discuss the effect of prenatal and birth events on personality and relationships. An excellent introduction to rebirthing.

Shapiro, Jerrold Lee, Ph.D. *When Men Are Pregnant.*
San Luis Obispo, California: Impact Publishers, 1988.

The experiences of men during pregnancy are explored in depth. The book deals with issues men rarely hear about: the real doubts fathers entertain about pregnancy, the psychological pressures they are under during pregnancy, the casual treatment they often receive from the medical establishment.

Shettles, Landrum B. *From Conception to Birth.*
New York: Harper & Row, 1974.

Simkin, Penny. *The Birth Partner.*
Boston: The Harvard Common Press, 1989.

Shows how the birth partner can help a woman experience a meaningful and joyful birth.

Stern, Daniel N. *The Interpersonal World of the Infant.*
New York: Basic Books, 1985.

This landmark book is essential reading for clinicians, researchers, and anyone else interested in theoretical issues of human development. A scientist, psychoanalyst, and science writer, Stern argues that infants differentiate themselves almost from birth and progress through increasingly complex modes of relatedness. He challenges not only the traditionally accepted concepts of developmental sequence but also the notion that certain tasks are confined to infancy.

Verny, Thomas R., M.D., with John Kelly. *The Secret Life of the Unborn Child.*
New York: A Delta Book, Dell Publishing, 1986.

Describes groundbreaking research in the field of pre- and perinatal psychology. Based on solid research findings from physiology, embryology, audiology, psychology, and related sciences, and illustrated with memorable case histories, this book is an invaluable companion for would-be parents as well as for clinicians and academics. Called by the prestigious *Behavior Today* newsletter the "urtext" in the field, which Dr. Verny himself first delineated.

Verny, Thomas R., M.D., Editor. *Pre- and Peri-Natal Psychology: An Introduction.*
New York: Human Sciences Press, 1987.

A collection of eighteen papers presented at the First International Congress on Pre- and Perinatal Psychology, held in Toronto in 1983. An excellent survey of this exciting new frontier of psychology. Particularly recommended for students, clinicians, and researchers.

Verny, Thomas R., M.D. *Parenting Your Unborn Child.*
Toronto: Doubleday Canada, 1988.

This is really three books in one: a practical guide to a happy and healthy pregnancy, a diary, and a photographic album. By working through the book, parents will learn to communicate with each other and the growing baby. They will also provide for their child a most important record of his or her beginnings.

Wasserman, Selma. *The Long Distance Grandmother.*
Point Roberts, Washington: Hartley & Marks, 1988.

Provides many ingenious ways to bridge geographical distances between grandparents and their grandchildren, through letter writing, telephone calls, audiotapes, family chronicles, and the like. A useful book for all grandparents.

Williams, Phyllis S., R.N. *Nourishing Your Unborn Child.* New York: Avon Books, 1982.

Describes the essential nutrients and the foods that contain them as well as the role of vitamin and mineral supplements and what they do for you and your baby.

Journals and Periodicals

Birth
Blackwell Scientific Publications
3 Cambridge Center, Suite 208
Cambridge MA 02142

An interdisciplinary refereed journal for those who provide care to childbearing families and evaluate such care in epidemiologic, public-health, and comparative-culture terms.

Mothering
P.O. Box 1690
Santa Fe NM 87504

Published quarterly, this is one of the most informative, readable, and reliable publications for the nonprofessional. Highly recommended.

Pre- and Peri-Natal Psychology Journal
Human Sciences Press
233 Spring Street, New York NY 10013-1578

A quarterly publication of the Pre- and Peri-Natal Psychology Association of North America (PPPANA). The leading-edge scientific journal for readers interested in pre- and perinatal psychology. Presently in its sixth year of publication, it is an interdisciplinary and refereed journal.

Organizations and Associations

The American Society of Psychoprophylaxis in Obstetrics
ASPO/Lamaze
1840 Wilson Boulevard, #204
Arlington VA 22201

Promotes the Lamaze method of prepared childbirth and sponsors a nationally standardized teacher-certification program.

International Childbirth Education Association
P.O. Box 20048
Minneapolis MN 55420-0048

Unites individuals and groups who support family-centered maternity care and believe in freedom of choice based on knowledge of alternatives. Publishes a quarterly journal.

The International Society for Prenatal and Perinatal Psychology and Medicine (ISPPM)

Primarily a Western European organization dealing with issues of prenatal psychology, it convenes triennial conferences and publishes a journal. For more information write to the president, Dr. Peter Fedor-Freybergh, Engelbrektsgaten 19, 3tr., Stockholm S-11432, Sweden

La Leche League International (LLLI)
9616 Minneapolis Avenue
Franklin Park IL 60131

Has local chapters throughout the United States and Canada. It offers breast-feeding information and support groups.

National Association of Parents and Professionals for Safe Alternatives in Childbirth (NAPSAC)
P.O. Box 646
Marble Hill MO 63764

Supports and promotes safe alternatives in childbirth, with heavy emphasis on home births and opposition to unnecessary medical intervention. Publishes books and newsletters and occasionally holds conferences.

Pre- and Peri-Natal Psychology Association of North America (PPPANA)
2162 Ingleside Avenue
Macon GA 31204

An educational, nonprofit organization dedicated to the in-depth exploration of the psychological dimension of human reproduction and pregnancy and the mental and emotional development of the unborn and newborn child. It is open to all interested persons. The association holds biennial international congresses and publishes the *Pre- and Peri-Natal Psychology Journal.*

Videos and Audiocassettes

Ballard, Royda, B.S.N., M.S.N., and Kelley Ballard, R.N., M.S.N.
Knowing the Unborn (video, 29 minutes)
Pre-Birth Parenting, 2554 Lincoln Boulevard, Suite 509, Marina del Rey CA 90291

This twenty-nine-minute video is based on interviews that the authors/producers conducted at the Third International PPPANA Congress in San Francisco in 1987. It is an excellent introduction to the subject of the amazing unborn and the communication that exists between him/her and the pregnant mother. It is surely a reflection on the quality of this video that it is already being used in Lamaze and childbirth classes, a crisis pregnancy agency, and family life education programs in parochial schools.

Peterson, Gayle
Body Centered Hypnosis (video, 54 minutes)
Shadow & Light Productions, 1749 Vine Street, Berkeley CA 94703

Based on Peterson's relaxation and visualization exercises as first elucidated in her excellent book, *Birthing Normally.* Very helpful and easy to follow.

Thurman, Leon, and Anna Peter Langness
Heartsongs (audio, 60 minutes)
5000 Bloomington Avenue South, Minneapolis MN 55417

A most attractive package, including a booklet on theory and practice of parent-child communication and an audiocassette. Side one of the cassette offers information about the purpose of *Heartsongs* and why voice and singing are used to communicate with one's baby. Side two contains fourteen songs based on traditional folk songs. Verse options for both expectant and new parents are suggested.

Trout, Michael
The Awakening and Growth of the Human: Studies in Infant Mental Health (video, 30 minutes each)
The Infant-Parent Institute, 501 South Street, Champaign IL 61820

This series of five tapes is intended for clinicians, educators, and researchers. One tape discusses such issues as the ambivalence mothers feel at each pregnancy and birth, the psychological meaning of a new resident in the home, and the process by which the baby is gradually recognized as a separate individual. Another tape explains how real and imagined traits of the newborn affect the way that child is integrated into the family.

Uplinger, Laura
A Gift for the Unborn Child (video, 26 minutes)
Bradley Boatman Productions, P.O. Box 4141, Malibu CA 90265

One of the best videos ever made on prenatal psychology. Through interviews with leading experts, it blends information about the field with visual imagery and music.

Verny, Thomas R., M.D., and Sandra Collier, B.A.
Love Chords (audio, 40 minutes)
Birth & Life Bookstore, 7001 Alonzo Avenue, P.O. Box 70625, Seattle WA 98107-0625
In Canada: Tobin Productions, 36 Madison Avenue, Toronto ON, M5R 2S1

This audiotape features the works of Baroque and post-Baroque composers such as Vivaldi, Bach, and Telemann and is based on years of research by both authors. Enclosed is a Pregnancy Guide and baby growth chart. *Love Chords* induces the state of alert relaxation best suited for learning. Consequently, listening to the music will facilitate communication between parents and their unborn children. The music is meant to act as an emotional bridge between the pregnant mother, father, and unborn child. The Pregnancy

Guide provides practical, easy-to-follow exercises and suggestions for a conscious pregnancy.

Both *Heartsongs* and *Love Chords* are beautifully packaged and make ideal gifts for pregnant parents. While the former teaches parents how and what to sing to their babies, the latter presents classical music without any spoken language. Therefore, the two works may be used in conjunction with each other to fully enhance the development of the unborn.

REFERENCES

Month One

p. 3 Ostrander, Sheila, and Lynn Schroeder with Nancy Ostrander. *Superlearning.* New York: Dell Publishing, 1979, p. 73.

p. 4 Lozanov, Georgi. "The Nature and History of the Suggestopedic System of Teaching Foreign Languages and Its Experimental Prospects." *Suggestology and Suggestopedia Journal,* vol. 1, 1975.

Ostrander, Sheila, et al. *Superlearning*, pp. 63–76.

Clements, Michele. "Observations on Certain Aspects of Neonatal Behaviour with Response to Auditory Stimuli." The 5th International Congress of Psychosomatic Obstetrics and Gynecology, Abstracts, 1977.

p. 5 O'Connor, Joan. "Researchers Attempt to Solve Riddle of Sleep's Busy Brain." *Psychiatric News,* 16 Jan. 1987, pp. 17–18.

Pivik, R.T. "Sleep Research—Twenty Years Perspective." *The Psychiatric Journal of the University of Ottawa* 4 (No. 1): 57–63.

p. 10 Edwards, K.R., and R. Jones. "Personality Changes Related to Pregnancy." Proceedings, 78th Annual Convention American Psychology Association, 1970, p. 341.

Spielberg, C., and G. Jacobs. "Emotional Reactions to the Stress of Pregnancy" in *Emotion and Reproduction,* ed. L. Carenza and L. Zichella. London: Academic Press, 1979, p. 13.

Sontag, Lester W., quoted in Ashley Montagu, *Life Before Birth.* New York: New American Library, 1964, p. 50.

p. 23 Maybruck, Patricia. *Pregnancy and Dreams.* Los Angeles: Jeremy P. Tarcher, 1989.

p. 24 Patricia Maybruck, *Pregnancy and Dreams.*

Vinget, Carolyn, and Frederick T. Knapp. "The Relationship of the Manifest Content of Dreams to Duration of Labor in Primiparae." *Psychosomatic Medicine,* July–Aug. 1972, pp. 313–319.

p. 30 Siegel, Bernie S. *Love, Medicine and Miracles.* New York: Harper & Row, 1986.

Kabat-Zinn, Jon. *Full Catastrophe Living.* New York: Delacorte Press, 1990.

Simonton, O. Carl, Stephanie Matthews-Simonton, and James L. Creighton. *Getting Well Again.* New York: Bantam Books, 1980.

Suinn, Richard M. "Imagery Rehearsal Applications to Performance Enhancement," *The Behavior Therapist* 8 (1985):155–159; and "Visualization in Sports," in *Imagery in Sports,* ed. A. Sheikh. Amityville, N.Y.: Baywood Publishing, 1986.

p. 32 Rottman, Gerhard. "Untersuchungen uber Einstellung zur Schwangerschaft und zur fotalen Entwicklung." Geist und Psyche, *Prenatale Psychologie,* ed. Hans Graber. Munich: Kindler Verlag, 1974, pp. 68–87.

p. 36 Klauser, Henriette Anne. *Writing on Both Sides of the Brain.* San Francisco: Harper & Row, 1987.

Month Three

p. 51 Verny, Thomas R. with John Kelly. *The Secret Life of the Unborn Child.* New York: Dell Publishing, 1986.

Verny, Thomas R., ed. *Pre- and Peri-Natal Psychology: An Introduction.* New York: Human Sciences Press, 1987.

Chamberlain, David B. *Babies Remember Birth.* Los Angeles: Jeremy P. Tarcher, 1988.

p. 52 Salk, Lee, L. P. Lipsitt, W. Q. Sturner, B. M. Reilly, and R. H. Levat. "Relationship of maternal and perinatal conditions to eventual adolescent suicide." *Lancet,* 16 March 1985, pp. 624–627.

Bissell, Lewis. Panel discussion at PPPANA conference, 1989.

Jacobson, Bertil. "Perinatal Origin of Eventual Self-Destructive Behaviour," *Pre- and Peri-Natal Psychology Journal* 2 (No. 4, Summer 1988):227–241.

p. 53 Cheek, David B. "Sequential Head and Shoulder Movements Appearing with Age Regression in Hypnosis to Birth." *Annual*

Journal of Clinical Hypnosis 16 (No. 4, 1974):261–266.

p. 54 Chamberlain, David B. *Consciousness at Birth: A Review of the Empirical Evidence.* San Diego: Chamberlain Communications, 1983.

Mathison, Linda. "Does Your Child Remember?" *Mothering,* Fall 1981, pp 103–107.

Laibow, Rima, M.D., personal communication.

p. 57 Edwards, Betty. *Drawing on the Right Side of the Brain.* Los Angeles: Jeremy P. Tarcher, 1979, and *Drawing on the Artist Within,* New York: Fireside, 1986.

p. 68 Harary, Keith. "Womb With a View." *Omni,* vol. 11, no. 11, pp. 39–40 and 94–97.

Van de Carr, F. Rene, and Marc Lehrer. "Prenatal University: Commitment to Fetal-Family Bonding and the Strengthening of the Family Unit as an Educational Institution." *Pre- and Peri-Natal Psychology Journal* 3 (No. 2, 1988):87–102.

p. 71 Jung, C. G. *Mandala Symbolism,* Princeton, New Jersey: Princeton University Press, 1972.

Month Four

p. 79 Liley, A. W. "The Foetus as a Personality." *Australian and New Zealand Journal of Psychiatry* 6 (No. 2, 1972):99–105.

Spelt, D. K. "The Conditioning of the Human Fetus in Utero." *Journal of Experimental Psychology* 38 (1948):338–346.

Month Five

p. 103 Verny, Thomas R., with John Kelly. *Secret Life of the Unborn Child,* pp. 22–23.

p. 104 Hepper, Peter. "Fetal Soap Addiction." *Lancet,* 11 June 1988, pp. 1347–48.

DeCaspar, Anthony J., and William P. Fifer. "Of Human Bonding: Newborns Prefer Their Mothers' Voices." *Science,* 6 June 1980, pp. 1174–76.

p. 105 DeCasper, Anthony J., and P. A. Prescott. "Human Newborns' Perception of Male Voices: Preference, Discrimination, and Reinforcing Value." *Developmental Psychobiology* 17 (No. 5, 1984):481–91.

p. 114 Patricia Maybruck, *Pregnancy and Dreams.*

Month Six

p. 120 Harlow, Harry F. "Love in Infant Monkeys." *Scientific American,* June 1959, pp. 68–74.

Ludington-Hoe, Susan, with Susan K. Galant. *How to Have a Smarter Baby.* New York: Rawson Associates, 1985.

p. 122 Laversen, Niels. *It's Your Pregnancy.* New York: Simon & Schuster, 1987, pp. 359–61.

p. 127 Olkin, Sylvia Klein. *Positive Pregnancy Fitness.* Garden City Park, N.Y.: Avery Publishing Group, 1987.

p. 131 Patricia Maybruck. *Pregnancy and Dreams.*

Month Seven

p. 139 Spelt, D. K. "Conditioning of the Human Foetus," pp. 338–46.

Lieberman, Michael. "Gravida's Smoking Seen Handicap to Offspring." *Obstetrics–Gynecology News* 5 (No. 12, 15 June 1970):16.

p. 144 Kabat-Zinn, Jon. *Full Catastrophe Living.*

p. 145 Olkin, Sylvia Klein. "Pre-Natal Yoga, 'Inner Bonding' and Natural Birth." *Pre- and Peri-Natal Psychology Journal* (Winter 1986):160–67.

p. 148 Siegel, Bernie S. *Love, Medicine, and Miracles.*

Kabat-Zinn, Jon. *Full Catastrophe Living.*

p. 157 Harary, Keith, and Pamela Weintraub. *Lucid Dreams in 30 Days: The Creative Sleep Program.* New York: St. Martin's Press, 1989.

Month Eight

p. 168 Lederman, Reginald P., et al. "The Relationship of Maternal Anxiety, Plasma Catecholamines, and Plasma Cortisol to Progress in Labor." *American Journal of Obstetrics & Gynecology* 132 (1 Nov. 1970):495–500.

Knapp, Frederick T., et al. "Some Psychological Factors in Prolonged Labor Due to Inefficient Uterine Action." *Comprehensive Psychiatry* 4 (Feb. 1963):9–17.

Dauds, Anthony, and Spencer DeVault. "Maternal Anxiety During Pregnancy and Childbirth Abnormalities." *Psychosomatic Medicine* 24 (Feb. 1963):464–469.

p. 171 Olkin, Sylvia Klein. *Positive Pregnancy Fitness.*

INDEX